MEMORIZE THE MASS!

MEMORIZE THE MASS!

How to Know and Love the Mass as if Your Life Depended on It

Kevin Vost, Psy.D.

En Route Books & Media
5705 Rhodes Avenue, St. Louis, MO 63109
Contact us at contactus@enroutebooksandmedia.com
Find En Route online at http://www.enroutebooksandmedia.com

Cover design by TJ Burdick
Interior illustrations by Ted Schluenderfritz

Paperback ISBN: 978-1-63337-091-3
Hardback ISBN: 978-1-63337-092-0
E-book ISBN: 978-1-63337-093-7

LCCN: 2016936607

Printed in the United States of America

Contents

Preface: When One's Life Depends on the Mass

"As in all other times of crisis, we relied on our religious backgrounds to give us strength and to help us accept the sacrifice of our monastic existence. I went through the Mass each day in English and Latin, took spiritual communion, and meditated deeply."

Admiral Jeremiah Denton[1]

In early 2015, I was working on a book about the Stoic philosophers. While examining their ongoing modern-day influence, I told the story of James Stockdale, a U.S. Navy fighter pilot who was shot from the skies over North Vietnam on September 9, 1965, and would remain a prisoner of the North Vietnamese Communist army for more than seven years. He attributed his success in holding up mentally to repeated bouts of torture and isolation and in giving solace to his fellow American POWs to his previous immersion in the ancient Stoic wisdom of the philosopher Epictetus. Epictetus taught that to maintain emotional tranquility, grow in virtue, and conform our will to God's, it is essential to distinguish between what we can and cannot control. Sometimes what we can control is little beyond

1 Admiral Jeremiah A. Denton, *When Hell Was in Session* (Washington, DC: WorldNetDaily, 1998), 189.

our own mental judgments, attitudes, and moral purpose. We must focus our efforts on those things we can control and endure with dignity events that are not up to us. Stockdale strove to control his own moral purpose and state of mind, since so little else was left up to him. He survived the ordeal and later became an admiral and the vice presidential running mate with Ross Perot in the 1992 presidential elections.

In the midst of writing that book,[2] I received an email from Major Valpiani, a U.S. Air Force officer and experimental test pilot. He had read one of my books on the memory techniques of Sts. Albert the Great and Thomas Aquinas, and he asked me if I could give him suggestions on how to memorize the parts of the Mass. You see, he had found through the Internet that I'd written an article called "Memorize the Mass!" on a now defunct Catholic social media site, and he wondered if I could share it with him. I remembered the article but found that my Word program didn't!

I was unable to track down the article for him, but I told him that I remembered the basics and could share those with him. What intrigued me about his email, however, was the story behind his question.

Major Valpiani had heard a recording of a talk from a man who had mentally repeated the Mass every day to preserve his sanity and sanctity during nearly eight years of confinement, also as a POW in North Vietnam, like Stockdale. That man, Jeremiah Denton, had been Commanding Officer of Attack Squadron Seventy-Five aboard the USS Independence and was shot down on July 18, 1965, two months before James Stockdale. His ordeal as a POW lasted nearly eight years. He, like Stockdale, later became an admiral, and then he became a U.S. senator from Alabama. I responded to the major that I had not heard of Admiral Denton but had, coincidentally, just written about Admiral Stockdale. In his response he told me that in fact the two were friends! That was news to me. Stockdale had not mentioned Denton in the books I'd read. Admiral Denton's story

2 Kevin Vost, *The Porch and the Cross: Ancient Stoic Wisdom for Modern Christian Living* (Kettering, OH: Angelico Press, 2016).

was clearly one that I had to investigate.

Sure enough, in his book *Hell is in Session*, Denton described how he and Stockdale cooperated in keeping the American POWs alive and in preserving their dignity. He described as well, in the quotation that started this preface, that throughout those years, many of which included solitary confinement and a variety of ongoing tortures, he did indeed go through the Mass each day in his head, both in English and in Latin!

Well, not long after this interchange, a Maryknoll missionary priest came to my parish and told the story of Bishop James Walsh, who was imprisoned in Communist China for nearly twelve years (1958-1970). Though he could not actually celebrate the Mass, the Mass and the Rosary gave him strength throughout his years of imprisonment. Indeed, so great was his love for the Mass that in the bishop's book *Zeal for Your House,* one photo shows him just after his release, still in a hospital bed, joyfully celebrating the Holy Mass for the first time after so many years, whilst still in his pajamas!

To keep a short preface from becoming long, these stories made it quite clear to me that providing a simple means of "memorizing the Mass," coming to know all of its parts, both backward and forward, would well be worth not just another article, but an entire book. Thankfully, Dr. Sebastian Mahfood and Shaun McAfee at En Route Books and Media agreed.

As much as the lives of Admiral Denton and Bishop Walsh depended on the Mass under such extreme crises, in a way, *all our lives depend upon it.* After all, the Eucharist is the heart of the Mass, and the *Catechism of the Catholic Church* makes clear that the Eucharist is "the source and summit of the Christian life" (1324).

The goal then of this book is to help you, reader, through the implementation of specialized memory methods recommended and employed by Sts. Albert the Great and Thomas Aquinas, to more fully and deeply experience that source and summit by writing the Holy Sacrifice of the Mass on the tablet of your heart.

Introduction: The Catholic Art of Memory Meets the Holy Sacrifice of the Mass

"The Sacrifice (of the Mass) is celebrated with many solemn rites and ceremonies, none of which should be deemed useless or superfluous. On the contrary, all of them tend to display the majesty of this august Sacrifice, and to excite the faithful when beholding these saving mysteries, to contemplate the divine things which lie concealed in the Eucharistic Sacrifice."
Catechism of the Council of Trent[1]

"Nothing that you have seen or heard is useful, however, unless you deposit what you should see and hear in the treasury of your memory."
St. Jerome[2]

The Mass is the heart of Catholic life, and the Eucharist is that heart's flesh and blood, the flesh and blood, soul and divinity of our Savior Jesus Christ. Christ initiated the Eucharist for us nearly two thousand years ago, and the Church has been greatly blessed by it and by the rites of the Holy

1 *Catechism of the Council of Trent for Parish Priests*, trans. John A. McHugh and Charles J. Callan (Rockford, IL: TAN Books, 1982), 276.

2 Cited in Mary Carruthers, *The Book of Memory: A Study of Memory in Medieval Culture* (Cambridge: Cambridge University Press, 1990), 18.

Sacrifice that so quickly grew around it to perfect it as the Church's ultimate act of worship.

The Holy Sacrifice of the Mass has four main ends or goals: adoration, thanksgiving, reparation, and prayer. The first end of the Mass is to honor and glorify God. The second end is to give Him thanks, to show gratitude for the countless benefits he has bestowed upon us, including our very existence. Indeed, the word Eucharist itself comes from the Greek eucaristα meaning "thankfulness." The third end is to obtain remission of the many venial sins we have made against God, atoning for our petty, ungrateful thoughts, desires, words, and deeds. The fourth end is to obtain earthly and eternal benefits and graces for ourselves and others through petitionary prayer.

As great as these ends are, the Mass is also a foretaste of heaven on earth and, indeed, it brings Christ Himself from heaven right into our midst in his sacramental, Eucharistic presence. Truly, there is nothing else to compare with the treasure we have in the likes of the Holy Mass.

Like the Back of Your Hand

Many of us adult Catholics have attended Mass for decades and have experienced it hundreds, if not thousands of times. Surely we've seen and held a simple penny countless times too, yet how many of us could accurately draw its details from memory? For that matter, could you right now, draw from memory the lines of your own palms, or even the veins on the back of your hands? After all, a common idiom indicating that someone has mastered some subject is to say that he knows it "like the back of his hand." Yet, how well do we really know the backs of our own hands, despite the countless times we have seen them? Even more so, regardless of how many Masses we've attended, how well do we really know the Mass? How well do we know the histories of the various prayers, their origins in the Bible and in Church Tradition, the reasons for our various gestures and postures, not to mention the origin and order of the various parts or rites of the Mass?

We are called to actively participate in the Mass, and this is one of the reasons we were presented with the New Order of the Mass that was promulgated by Pope Paul VI in 1969, published in Latin in 1970, and then translated into vernacular languages throughout the world. The New Order of the Mass was designed to provide more participation from Mass-goers in terms of vocal prayers, responses, readings, and more. Though we may be more *outwardly* active now than in the Traditional Latin Mass, we do need to ask ourselves if we are truly participating more on the *inside*, through our focused attention and understanding of the rites in which we are participating.

Well, the end or goal of this book is to assist you in better attaining all the ends of the Mass, to better praise God, to more sincerely repent of our sins, to better give Him thanks, and to ever more devoutly present our petitions before him, by a far greater internal participation in the Holy Sacrifice Christ gave us. The text and illustrations have been structured in such a way that, if you read slowly and carefully, look at the pictures, and follow the detailed step-by-step instructions, by the time you finish, you will be able to name and remember all of the thirty-two parts of the *Novus Ordo,* or Ordinary Form of the Roman Rite of the Mass, from the introductory rites, to the Liturgy of the Word, to the Liturgy of the Eucharist, to the Communion Rite, all the way through to each and every part of the concluding rites. And all of these parts are in their exact order, both forward and backward!

You will also be shown how to use your new memory skills to recall all forty-two parts of the Extraordinary Form of the Mass, known by many as the Traditional Latin Mass, a beautiful and still valid form that has endured with only minor changes for nearly two millennia. You will remember all the rites and their Latin names, including the Mass of the Catechumens, the Mass of the Faithful, the Canon of the Mass, the Rites of

Consecration and Communion, and the post-Communion rites including the last Gospel. These too you will come to know literally forward and backward, from 1 to 42 and from 42 back to 1. Now talk about knowing something *better than* the back of your hand!

The Catholic Art of Memory

Plain as day within the written works of two of the best known and greatest Catholic Doctors of the Church, Sts. Albert the Great and St. Thomas Aquinas, lies what we might call a "Catholic Art of Memory," and yet most of our modern world seems to have forgotten it! During the thirteenth century in their work as philosophers, theologians, and university professors, Sts. Albert and Thomas carefully examined, explained, and endorsed an ancient system of memory improvement, invented, it was said, by the Greek poet Simonides of Ceos (556-468 BC), and passed on to the Latin West primarily through the works of Marcus Tullius Cicero (107-43 BC). It became known in the West as "the method of loci" (*loci* being the Latin plural for locations). Not only did Albert and Thomas expound upon and endorse this memory method, they integrated or synthesized the ancient literature on *memory improvement* with Aristotle's writings on *the nature of human memory*, not only showing that the memory method works but also shedding light on why it is so effective.

It is not entirely surprising, however, that Sts. Albert and Thomas's method was all but forgotten. One event that likely played a large role was Guttenberg's invention of the printing press around the year 1440, one hundred and sixty years after St. Albert's death. With easy access to printed materials, a powerful memory perhaps no longer seemed so essential. It also did not help that many of Albert's writings have not been translated into vernacular languages from their Latin, and even though St. Thomas's *Summa theologica* has been widely translated and circulated throughout the centuries, it is a book of over three thousand pages, and his article on the memory method takes up only about one page, almost in the very middle![3]

It is there in his question entitled "Whether Memory is a Part of Prudence?" that Thomas explains and recommends the method in a way that may not be entirely clear if one has not been exposed, as he and his readers were, to the ancient art of "artificial" (man-made) memory.[4] St. Thomas had a tremendous gift for penetrating into the heart of any matter that came under the laser-like light of his lofty intellect. Here is how he summarized the four main features of that ancient art of memory:

There are four things whereby a man perfects his memory:

- First, when a man wishes to remember a thing, he should take *some suitable yet unwonted illustration of it,* since the unwonted strikes us more, and so makes a greater and stronger impression on the mind.
- Secondly, whatever a man wishes to retain in his memory he must carefully consider to *put in order*, so that he may pass easily from one memory to another.
- Thirdly, we must be *anxious and earnest* about the things we wish to remember, because the more a thing is impressed on the mind, the less it is liable to slip out of it.
- Fourthly, we should *often reflect* on the things we wish to remember... Wherefore when we reflect on a thing frequently, we quickly call it to mind, through passing from one thing to another by a kind of natural order (II-II, Q. 49, art. 1, numbers and emphasis added.)

So, in a nutshell that will soon mature into the full-grown oak of ar-

3 St. Thomas Aquinas, *Summa theologica*, II-II, q. 49, a. 1.

4 I have provided more extensive discussions of St. Thomas's role in the art of memory in *Memorize the Faith! (And Most Anything Else): Using the Methods of the Great Catholic Medieval Memory Masters* (Manchester, NH: Sophia Institute Press, 2006), and of St. Albert's role in *Memorize the Reasons! Defending the Faith with the Catholic Art of Memory* (El Cajon, CA: Catholic Answers, 2013). I'll provide just a very terse summary here, but enough for our purposes.

tificial memory, Thomas recommends that we form mental *images*, place them in a certain *order*, *concentrate* on them intently, and *rehearse* or *repeat* them often. Seven hundred years and at least as many scientific studies later, any honest modern memory training expert will have to admit that St. Thomas Aquinas got it right!

We will see very clearly how those four elements of images, order, concentration and repetition will enable us to memorize the parts of the Mass, both in the Ordinary (New Vernacular) and Extraordinary (Traditional Latin) Forms of the Mass, because *this book will include a step-by-step, fully guided tutorial in the use and the mastery of this memory system as applied to both forms of the Mass.*

Sometimes Silly Images: Always Sacred Rites

One thing to bear in mind as we apply this memory method to the parts of the Holy Mass is that while the memory images we use will oftentimes seem odd, humorous, and grossly exaggerated, the rites of the Mass that they hold in mind for us are always holy and sacred. We will keep at the forefronts of our minds that as the map is not the territory, our sometimes silly images are not the always sacred rites they represent.

Admiral Denton, while prisoner in North Vietnam, made headlines around the world when during a film produced by his Communist captors for their propaganda purposes, he stealthily revealed to the world that the POWs were indeed being tortured, by using his eyes to blink out the word "torture" in Morse code! So crafty too were he and his men that when transported in vehicles together while forbidden to talk, they communicated to each other by tapping on their neighbor's knees with their knees, again, in Morse code!

In a somewhat similar way, the memory images we will use are but a code for the deep truths they represent and call to mind. Further, the images need to be striking, because that is how our memory works. St. Thomas himself states that even spiritual ideas are best remembered through images of physical things "because human memory has a greater hold on sensible objects." Further, in referring to using "unwonted" illustrations, Thomas uses the Latin word *miramur* to describe these images – things at which we marvel or wonder. St. Albert, echoing the oldest extant memory improvement treatise, the *ad Herennium,* long attributed to Cicero, explicitly advised that these memory images be made "as striking as possible," to picture them "doing something" and having "exceptional beauty or ugliness."[5]

We are bombarded every day with so many countless impressions that we naturally remember best what is most unusual and striking. Those are the kinds of events that we might say impress our memories, making a firm impression upon them. Of course Christ Himself was also well aware of the use of colorful stories and images in helping learn spiritual lessons. He taught, after all, in parables and was no stranger at all to colorful phrases, from a camel passing through the eye of a needle to the straining out a gnat and the swallowing of a camel (Matt 19:24; 23:24)!

So, these images, though unusual and light-hearted, will present us with no "Clown Mass" or anything of the sort. They do nothing to counter the sacredness of the rites of the Mass themselves. Further, I assure you that after you have thoroughly mastered the parts of the Mass with this method, you will find over time that you'll know the parts in order even without the images. Our goal, after all, is to write the Mass on the tablets of our hearts.

The Holy Sacrifice of the Mass

To come to better know and love the Holy Mass is indeed the end or goal of this book, and the memory methods are but the means. The Mass is a most beautiful thing that has developed over the course of nearly two millennia. As I guide you through the memory method tutorials in

5 From *De Bono* (On the Good), cited in Carruthers, *The Book of Memory,* 275.

each chapter of this book, please bear in mind that the numerical ordering system I use is to some extent arbitrary. The memory method requires a numbering system to lock things in their exact order (as you'll see it does so well), but the arbitrariness lies in the fact that you will find thirty-two parts for the *Novus Ordo* Mass and forty-two for the Traditional Latin Mass.[6] I use thirty-two for the New Mass because that is how the holy rites are numbered in the *St. Joseph Sunday Missal* that I personally use.[7] I use forty-two parts for the New Mass because, at first unable to find a comparably numbered missal for the Tridentine Mass, I simply followed the helpful section headings in Dom Prosper Gueranger, O.S.B.'s *Explanation of the Holy Mass.*[8]

As you will come to see, each of those "parts" may include a series of gestures and more than one prayer, or prayers with more than one part.[9] Further, I will note that true mastery of all of the holy rites of the Mass is truly the province of only a thoroughly trained and ordained priest. There is so much to the Mass that I can barely scratch the surface here, but it is a surface so worth the scratching. My expert role here is not of course as priest or as theologian, but as a master of memory method who relies for his content on saints and theologians faithfully aligned with the glorious Magisterium of the Holy Catholic Church. In that regard I will make clear as well that the

6 I should note as well that I will use the terms *Novus Ordo,* "New Mass," and "Ordinary Form of the Mass" interchangeably to refer to the Mass Pope Blessed Paul VI promulgated in 1970, and the terms "Traditional Latin Mass," "Tridentine Mass," or "Extraordinary Form of the Mass" for the Mass that Pope St. Pius V promulgated in 1570 and which last appeared in the 1962 edition during the pontificate of Pope St. John XXIII.

7 *New Saint Joseph Sunday Missal: Complete Edition* (New Jersey: Catholic Book, 2011).

8 Dom Prosper Gueranger, *Explanation of the Prayers and Ceremonies of the Holy Mass: Taken from Notes Made at the Conferences of Dom Prosper Gueranger, Abbot of Solesmes* (Fitzwilliam, NH: Loreto, 2007).

9 I have since obtained the *Daily Missal and Liturgical Manual for the Roman Missal and Breviary, 1962* (London: Baronius Press, 2014) and it does contain a numbered sequence of the Ordinary of the Mass on pages 898-899. They have numbered thirty-six parts, though five of those parts have lettered subparts that would add another fourteen parts to a memory tour. I think you will find that our forty-two parts parallel those pretty closely and lead to a satisfactory mastery of the parts of the Latin Mass.

wording for the prayers of the Mass comes from *The Roman Missal*.[10]

Memoria Verborum/Memoria Rerum

As you complete the memory tours of this book for the first time, you will by no means master all of the words of each of the prayers, unless you already knew them. Even the ancient Roman memory masters distinguished between what they called *memoria verborum* (memory for words) and *memoria rerum* (memory for things). The ancient art of memory we are applying here is *not* best suited for memory for words, that is, word-for-word rote memorization of the exact wording or texts or prayers. It may be used to assist in such verbatim memorization if difficulties arise in a particular part of a particular prayer, but its main function lies within the realm of *memoria rerum,* memory for things, and those "things" we will remember are the most important "things" in the world: the names, sequence, and significance of the holy rites of the Mass. Through weekly, (ideally daily), attendance at Mass, those prayers too, if not yet memorized, will work their way as well into the treasuries of our memory, if you pay close *attention* to them and *repeat* them again and again and again.[11]

I will note as well that while this book may be read on its own and used as an aid for Mass, if you are not already well-versed in the Mass at the start (especially the Latin Mass), you would do very well to use this book to supplement a formal missal, while you read it at home and while actually present at Mass. If the missal is your personal copy and is not already numbered, it may be of help to neatly add the numbers in pencil

10 *The Roman Missal* © 2010, International Commission on English in the Liturgy Corporation. All rights reserved.

11 Recall, if you will, that *concentration* and *repetition* are themselves two of the four things that, according to St. Thomas, perfect the human memory. As for the specialized methods of *images* and *order* you will find in the pages ahead, while they too still require focused concentration and repeated efforts, I think you will find them effective, and as some readers of my previous memory books have noted, even *fun* as well, for it seems that our modern-day neglected memory muscles actually relish a challenging workout!

at the start of the appropriate parts in your missal. I found this a huge help in grasping, retaining, and better appreciating the Traditional Latin Mass. If all goes as planned, these methods will help your missal come alive for you, resonating with more meaning and helping you further write in your heart the holy treasures of the Holy Mass.

Without further ado then, let's forge on ahead and actually begin to memorize the Mass as if our very lives depended on it.

–Part I–

Writing the New Mass on the Tablet of Your Heart

"My son, do not forget my teaching, but let your heart keep my commandments... write them on the tablet of your heart."
Prov 3:1 & 3

"A thing is said metaphorically to be written in the mind of anyone when it is firmly held in memory."
St. Thomas Aquinas, *Summa theologiae*[1]

"Grant to me keenness of mind,
capacity to remember,
skill in learning, subtlety to interpret,
and eloquence of speech.
May you guide the beginning of my work,
direct its progress,
and bring it to completion."
From St. Thomas's prayer
Ante Studium ("Before Study")[2]

---

1 *ST*, I, q. 24, a.1, explicating Prov 3:3.

2 St. Thomas Aquinas, The Aquinas Prayer Book: *The Prayers and Hymns of Saint Thomas Aquinas*, trans. Robert Anderson and Johann Moser (Manchester, NH: Sophia Institute Press, 2000).

Introductory Rites

"[I]t is the business of the wise man to order. The reason for this is that wisdom is the most powerful perfection of reason whose characteristic is to know order...Now a twofold order is found in things. One kind is that of parts of a totality, that is, a group, among themselves, as the parts of a house are mutually ordered to each other. The second order is that of things to an end. This order is of greater importance than the first."
St. Thomas Aquinas[3]

"As for me and my household, we will serve the LORD."
Joshua 24:15

Welcome (Back) to the House of Memory!

I include the "back" in parenthesis for those who have already been guests to my memory house within the pages of *Memorize the Faith!* We're delighted to have you over once more to see all the new and wonderful things that now lie within these walls. Though this house houses the "New Order" of the Mass, the literal "order" of the memory places within

3 St. Thomas Aquinas, Commentary on Aristotle's *Nicomachean Ethics* (Notre Dame: Dumb Ox Books, 1993), 1.

this house will remain almost exactly the same, as it will in Part II when we go through it once more to write within our hearts the Traditional Latin Mass. Of course, first time guests to this house are gladly and equally welcomed. You need not at all have been here before, for we'll happily guide you through every part of every room, never once leaving your side. And as we begin we will keep our *end* clearly in mind: that the parts of this memory house will help you recall the order and meaning of the parts of the Holy Mass.

Before we begin our memory tour, I invite you to turn your powers of concentration and imagination as high as they will go since, after all, we are going to try to remember the noblest and highest sacrificial prayer and liturgical work of the Holy Catholic Church.

Imagine, if you will, that you have arrived at my house, a rather sprawling ranch-style home, nestled beneath the towering leafy canopies of old maples and oaks. You stride up to my front door (location 1) and ring the bell. As soon as the door opens, you are carried within by *a group of jubilant singers.* Buoyed by their joy as you step inside, you feel within your heart that this is no ordinary earthly home. As you step in upon the doormat (location 2), you are not surprised to see the word *"Greetings!"* written on it, but you are surprised when *little arms* sprout out from the mat and they make *the sign of the cross.* Now you see *lips as well,* and the mat *calls out "Greetings!"* too.

Not sure what kind of house you are entering into, you take a quick glance out through a glass panel next to the front door (location 3) and things look normal enough out there in the front yard, except that in front of the sprinkling *lawn sprinkler* is a flashing neon sign with the words "*holy water.*" Back within the foyer you look at the back wall on the other side of the door (location 4) and you feel more at home, for mounted upon that wall are all your own favorite baseball team's *pennants.*[4]

4 In my own neck of the woods, they had better be for the St. Louis Cardinals or Chicago Cubs (or perhaps, with the bishop's permission, his own favorite team, the Chicago White Sox).

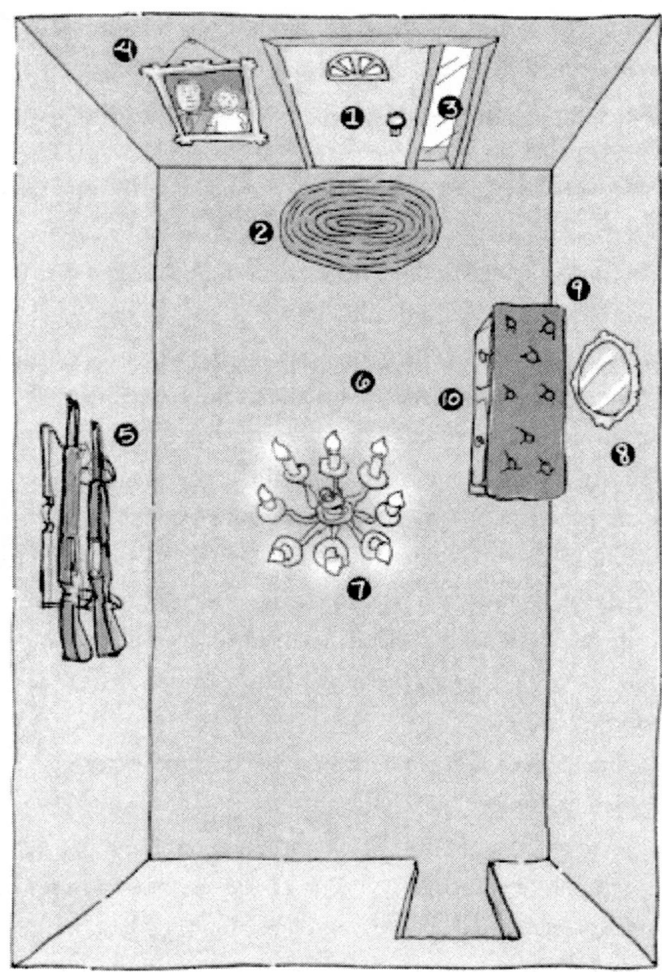

Foyer

There is a locked gun rack on the right wall[5] (location 5), and as you glance at it you swear you could hear striking strains of familiar symphonic music, of Richard Wagner in fact, for there are not rifles but swords and axes, and they're being replaced by sturdy, blonde warrior women! You are struck by the wings on their back. These are no ordinary women but in fact are the fabled *Valkyries.*[6] (Why are Valkyries in this foyer of the Holy Mass? Good question. That is just the kind of thing we explain later in this chapter.)

Moving back now to the center of the foyer (location 6), who should be standing there but that famous singer named *Gloria!* Not familiar with Gloria Gaynor or perhaps Gloria Estefan? No problem; place here any person you know who's named Gloria. Don't know any Glorias? Still no problem; just plant a U.S. flag there – a.k.a. "Old Glory." Our first chapter contains only one more location and image. Now, looking overhead at the chandelier (location 7) you see suspended upon it one of those church *collection baskets* on a stick. You can see that sticking out from the basket, however, are not dollar bills but *prayers written on slips of paper.*

Now, before we learn just what lofty rites have been symbolized by those silly images, let's make sure that we've actually memorized them. First, let's lay them out clearly:

LOCATION	IMAGE
1. Front door	*Jubilant singers enter*
2. Doormat	*Mat signs cross and calls out "Greetings!"*
3. Glass panel next to door	*Holy water sprinkler*

5 A remnant of its first use in Memorize the Faith! to remind readers of the Fifth Commandment, "Thou shalt not kill."

6 In ancient Norse mythology, these winged warriors roamed the fields of battle, deciding who would live or die, and carried the souls of the dead to Valhalla, the Viking warrior heaven of sorts. Perhaps Richard Wagner's most famous piece of music is his "Ride of the Valkyries." (Check it out online if you are not familiar.)

4. Back wall next to door	*Baseball pennants*
5. Gun rack	*Valkyries*
6. Center of foyer	*Singer or friend named Gloria (or "Old Glory")*
7. Chandelier	*Collection basket full of prayers*

Okay, now two more things.

First, let's recall that St. Thomas and other memory masters were very fond of repeating the saying *"repetitio est mater memoriae"* ("repetition is the mother of memory"). So, please take a minute or two and study the table above while visualizing the foyer in your mind's eye. See if you have memorized all the locations and images.

Second, let's recall that these memory methods were designed to master material *literally backward and forward.* So then, let's rehearse these locations and images one more time, this time, in their reverse order, from seven back to one.

Second Rehearse, Reverse of the First

As we retrace our steps though the memory foyer, can you work your way back through the collection basket full of prayers up in the chandelier (7), the person named Gloria (or "Old Glory") in the center of the foyer (6), the Valkyries at the gun rack (5), your team's pennants on the back wall (4) , the holy water sprinkler in the front yard (3), the doormat that called out a greeting (2), and the jubilant singers who came in through the front door (1)? Got, 'em? Good! If not, rehearse them once more and give it another try. When you have these seven locations and images locked in your mind, you will find that you locked down all seven parts of the introductory rites of the Mass as well. How so? I thought you'd never ask.

Let's see what we've really done here. Each of those seven strange visual images served to represent and remind us of one of the seven parts of the introductory rites of the Mass. The jubilant singers entering the door will remind us of the *entrance hymn*. It's not every day that a doormat actually greets you, but that was merely to remind us of the *greeting*, the second part of the Mass. That holy water sprinkler in the front yard was a pretty straightforward reminder of the *rite for the blessing and sprinkling of water* that takes place at this point, but only at certain times, as we'll explain in the pages ahead. Those pennants will surely remind us of the *penitential rite* that comes next, right before not Valkyries but the *Kyrie*. As easy as could be, Gloria or Old Glory reminds us of the *Gloria*. And last but not least, that collection box of prayers will remind us of that prayer of the priest known as the *Collect*. So now, let's lay it all out to see what you've really remembered.

LOCATION	***IMAGE***	**PART OF THE MASS**
1. Front door	*Jubilant singers enter*	Entrance hymn
2. Doormat	*Mat signs cross and calls out "Greetings!"*	Greeting
3. Glass panel next to door	*Holy water sprinkler*	Rite for the blessing and sprinkling of holy water
4. Back wall next to door	*Baseball pennants*	Penitential rite
5. Gun rack	*Valkyries*	*Kyrie*

6. Center of foyer	*Singer or friend named Gloria (or "Old Glory")*	*Gloria*
7. Chandelier	*Collection basket full of prayers*	Collect

If all has gone well, you now know the names of the first seven parts of the Ordinary Form of the Mass in their exact order. The *names* of these rites are important in themselves, but they are certainly just the tip of the iceberg when it comes to the depth of their history and meaning. We'll spend the rest of this chapter plummeting their depths just a bit so that we will not only *memorize* the parts of the Mass, but dive into deeper levels of *understanding* that will help us *discover*, better *appreciate*, and *participate* in treasures that were never meant to be sunken and buried below the conscious awareness of Christ-loving Mass-goers.

1. Entrance Hymn

In our memory tour, you entered the front door of the house (location 1) and were swept away by jubilant singers to represent in the imagination what happens in reality after you enter the holy doors of a church for the celebration of Mass. You have entered the church reverently; dipped your fingers in the holy water font; crossed yourself in the name of the Father, and of the Son, and of the Holy Spirit; genuflected on your right knee as you entered the pew (or bowed if you are physically unable); and now, after kneeling a few moments in silent prayer, you rise and stand as the Mass itself begins. Those singers represent the entrance hymn, chant, or song—part of the opening procession. Our job in the pews is to sing along, even if off-key or silently. Indeed, if we feel shy or perhaps unmoved by the particular hymn that was chosen today, we can still offer up our minor discomfort and recall that this song is sung not to please us but to praise

God. As we sing a crucifix is held aloft by an altar server, followed typically by another server (a deacon, if present) and the presiding priest. We sing our praises to God as they proceed to the altar, all bowing before it, while the deacon and priest bend to kiss the holy altar, a symbol of Christ Himself.

Consider, if you will, that in countless places across the world, *at this very moment* and at *every moment* for nearly two thousand years, a different priest and a different congregation are and have been preparing to celebrate this very same holy sacrifice. So then, when you recall our first memory image, let it trigger a sense of the holiness and reverence for what has begun, and heartfelt gratitude to God that we have been called to participate in it.

2. Greeting

A doormat (location 2) is a pretty straightforward reminder for a greeting, and this particular greeting from the presiding priest in the sanctuary at the front of the church begins with a sign of the cross. "In the name of the Father, and of the Son, and of the Holy Spirit," he says, and we, of course, answer, "Amen." The priest's sign of the cross proclaims the Trinity and reminds us of the cross of Christ's Passion and the great commission he gave his disciples to go and "make disciples of all nations, baptizing them in the name of the Father, and of the Son and of the Holy Spirit" (Matt 28:19).[7]

Our "Amen" harks back to the worship of the ancient Hebrews, for it is the Hebrew word for "truth" or "certainty" and has been used by Christians for millennia in Mass as a powerful affirmation, meaning "truly," "verily," or "so be it!" We should say it not as two mindless syllables we've utter countless times, but mindfully, joyfully, and with gusto and conviction. This is the first of many "Amens" we will utter in Mass, and for centuries it has been among the most notable hallmarks of Christian worship. Indeed, in

7 The sign of the cross is not typically used as a part of Protestant prayer. I can only wonder how many non-Catholics who find the sign of the cross strange or foreign realize that the words are certainly no mere "tradition of men," but indeed directly quote Jesus Christ himself!

one of the ancient lives of St. Patrick, apostle to the Irish, a fifth century Druid priest forewarns the pagan King Laeghaire Mac Neill of a prophetic vision he's had of a new faith that would arrive and live forever in Erin (i.e., Ireland), describing it like this:

> A *Tailecend* (*i.e.,* Patrick) shall come across the stormy sea.
> His garment head-pierced, his staff head-bent,
> His *mias* *(i.e.,* altar) in the east of his house;
> His people all shall answer, Amen, amen.[8]

When we utter our own "Amens," perhaps we can reflect from time to time that we are joining the chorus of the countless "Amens" across time and across nations, recited in every accent imaginable to affirm that great new faith in the Holy Trinity that St. Patrick and multitudes of great saints like him have gone to such great costs to spread unto the ends of the earth—indeed, all the way to our very own parish!

The priest then welcomes us to Mass using one of these three forms of greeting: (a) "The grace of our Lord Jesus Christ, and the love of God, and the communion of the Holy Spirit be with you all," (b) "Grace to you and peace from God our Father and the Lord Jesus Christ," or simply (c) "The Lord be with you" (or "Peace be with you," if the celebrant is a bishop). And we answer, "And with your spirit."[9]

---

8 James O'Leary, ed., *The Most Ancient Lives of St. Patrick* (St. Augustine Academy Press, 2010), 36.

9 As for their direct biblical bases, option A uses the words of 2 Corinthians 13-14, option B, 1 Corinthians 1:3, and option C, Ruth 2:4 for the priest's greeting, and John 20:26 for the bishop's. The response "and with your spirit" echoes St. Paul's words in Galatians 6:18 and 2 Timothy 4:22. (Some people call their non-Catholic Christian churches a "Bible church" or a "Bible-based church." Anyone who might think that the Catholic Church does not have the most profound of biblical roots needs merely to pay close attention during virtually any part of any Catholic Mass! Still, we should bear in mind that in a sense the Mass is even pre-biblical, for the New Testament anyway, since the apostles promulgated the Mass around the world three centuries before the canon of the New Testament was established once and for all by the Catholic Church.)

So then, we have all gathered together; sung a hymn of praise to God; honored the Trinity; remembered Christ's cross and our call to evangelize; been welcomed by the priest; and prayed that God's grace, love, and peace be with the spirits of the priest and all those gathered for Mass. That's quite a bit in just the first couple of minutes, but we need to move along to see what may (or may not) happen next.

3. Rite for the Blessing and Sprinkling of Holy Water

We saw that holy water sprinkler in the front yard (location 3) to remind us of this rite that is performed next if Mass is being celebrated on certain Sundays in Easter time and particularly at Pentecost. Here, in the rite of blessing and sprinkling of holy water, the priest circulates throughout the nave of the church, sprinkling the congregation with holy water using either an *aspergillum* (a sacrament instrument of metal with holes at the end that is a literal holy water sprinkler) or a hyssop branch. The rite and the instrument derive their name and meaning from Psalm 50:9 in the Latin Vulgate, *"Asperges me hyssopo et mundabor; lavabis me et super nivem dealbabor"*: "Cleanse me with hyssop, that I may be pure; wash me, and I will be whiter than snow" (Ps 51:7). The sprinkling is a reminder of our baptism and renewal of our baptismal promise. The priest stands over the vessel holding the water and recites one of three prayers that ask for God's blessing upon the water as a memorial of our baptism that cleansed us of sin and opened to us the spring of God's graces unto our salvation. Again, we answer, "Amen."

4. Penitential Rite

Throughout the majority of the church calendar, we move not from the greeting to the sprinkling rite but to the penitential rite (hence our pennants on the wall of location 4). Here, we acknowledge our sins and ask for God's mercy and forgiveness. The priest calls us to repentance: "Brethren (brothers and sisters), let us acknowledge our sins, and so prepare ourselves to celebrate the sacred mysteries." Next, after a brief pause for silent reflection, the priest commences with one of three possible penitential prayers.

The first option is the ancient prayer known as the *"Confiteor,"* the Latin word for "I confess," which are the first words of this prayer. Both the priest and the people pray as follows:

I confess to almighty God
and to you, my brothers and sisters,
that I have greatly sinned,
in my thoughts and in my words,
in what I have done and in what I have failed to do,
through my fault, through my fault,
through my most grievous fault;
therefore I ask blessed Mary ever-Virgin,
all the Angels and Saints,
and you, my
brothers and sisters,
to pray for me to the Lord our God.

The second option is as follows:

Priest: Have mercy on us, O Lord.
People: For we have sinned against you.
Priest: Show us, O Lord, your mercy.
People: And grant us your salvation.

The third option for the penitential prayer is below:

Priest or Deacon: You were sent to heal the contrite of heart: Lord have mercy.

People: Lord have mercy.

Priest or Deacon: You came to call sinners; Christ have mercy.

People: Christ have mercy.

Priest or Deacon: You are seated at the right hand of the Father to intercede for us: Lord have mercy.

People: Lord, have mercy.

Finally, at the conclusion of any of the three forms of the penitential prayer, the priest prays aloud, "May almighty God have mercy on us, forgive us our sins, and bring us to everlasting life," to which we again answer, "Amen."

Both the Old and New Testaments are full of examples of and exhortations to the public and private confession of sins.[10] Further, St. Paul exhorts us when explicitly referring to the Eucharist: "A person should examine himself" (1 Cor 11:28), lest he or she eat the bread and drink of the cup unworthily. So, in the *Confiteor*—the first penitential prayer—we examine our consciences for the various ways we have sinned in thought, word, and deed—in the bad things we did and in the good things we did not do—and we show sincere contrition as evidenced by the fact that we emphasize our personal responsibility for our own faults three times, each time beating our breast in that ancient symbol of sorrow and mourning, as we saw when the crowd who had witnessed Christ's Crucifixion "returned home beating their breasts" (Luke 23:48).

The two other briefer options for the penitential prayer are explicitly scriptural in their origins. The second option draws from Baruch 3:2, "Here, LORD, and have mercy, for you are a merciful God; have mercy

10 Lev 5:5, Num 5:7, Neh 1:6 & 9:2, Ps 32:5, 38:18, Prov 28:13, Sir 4:26, Dan 9:20, Matt 3:6, Mark 1:5, 1 John 1:9, and Jas 5:16 are examples cited by Edward Sri in *A Biblical Walk Through the Mass: Understanding What We Say and Do in the Liturgy* (West Chester, PA: Ascension Press, 2011), 31-32.

on us who have sinned against you." And our response draws from Psalm 85:7, "Show us LORD your mercy; grant us your salvation."

The third option draws from Isaiah 61, which proclaims the liberating message of the Messiah. The priest's second declaration in this penitential prayer draws from Matthew 9:13: "'I desire mercy, not sacrifice.' I did not come to call the righteous, but sinners," and his third from Romans 8:34: "It is Christ [Jesus] who died, rather, was raised, who is also at the right hand of God, who intercedes for us."

Whichever option has been used, the priest concludes with this absolution: "May almighty God have mercy on us, forgive us our sins, and bring us to everlasting life," to which we answer, yet again, "Amen."

5. Kyrie

And now you heard those stirring strains of Wagner when at the gun rack in the foyer (location 5) you saw the flight of the Valkyries. Now we examine the phrase or the song you really do hear at Mass, because it is time for the *Kyrie*. (Indeed, we might as well imagine those Valkyries praying the *Kyrie* too!) Unless the third option (which includes the *Kyrie Eleison*) was used for the penitential rite, now we sing or say the *Kyrie* as follows:

Priest or cantor: Lord, have mercy.
People: Lord, have mercy.
Priest or Cantor: Christ, have mercy.
People: Christ, have mercy.
Priest or Cantor: Lord, have mercy.
People: Lord, have mercy.

This prayer is called the *Kyrie* from its original ancient Greek, for "Kyrie" means "the Lord." The original Greek for "have mercy" is *"eleison,"* and sometimes this too will be chanted or sung in the Greek as *"Kyrie elesion; Christe, eleison; Kyrie eleison."*[11] The medieval Dominican theologian and teacher of St. Thomas Aquinas, St. Albert the Great, explained why the *Kyrie* was traditionally sung in Greek rather than in Latin. He elaborates on four reasons which are presented here in summary:

1. "First because it was in Greece that the most sublime wisdom flourished, as it is said in the Epistle to the Corinthians: 'The Jews require signs, and the Greeks seek after wisdom."
2. Second it was because of their observance of laws and natural justice, "for as the Jew recognized this justice of the Gospel through faith in the justice of the Mosaic law, so also the Greek discovered the justice of the Gospel through faith in natural justice."
3. The third reason relates to language. The majority of the New

11 *Christos* is the Greek for "Anointed One" or "Messiah." The words are pronounced as "kee-**ree**-eh ay-**lay**-ee-sohn"; "**Krees**-tay ay-**lay**-ee-sohn." (I cannot help but share with you what I'm hearing as I type these words. I recommend that sometime, through CD or through the Internet, you listen to the *Kyrie* of Catholic composer Anton Bruckner's Mass No. 1 in D Minor. I find the *Kyrie*, the *Agnus Dei*, and all of the prayers of this Mass rendered most hauntingly and reverently. For a more rousing version, try the *Kyrie* of Mozart's famous Requiem Mass. Indeed, many of the greatest classical composers including Beethoven, Tchaichovksy, and others, have written beautiful Masses that can be listened to with spiritual profit while you read about, memorize, and contemplate the Mass!)

Testament had been written in Greek, and the first seven churches were founded in the parts of Asia Minor called Greece.

4. The fourth reason is that the faith came to the Latins from Greece, whence Sts. Peter and Paul had travelled first. The words of the *Kyrie Eleison*, "Lord, have mercy," recall that the Greeks were the first of the Gentiles to receive from Paul and Barnabas the grace of salvation (Acts 13). "That this same grace was borne from Greece into the West, we preserve in the words and syllables which that people first used to implore the mercy of God."[12]

Whether we sing or chant the words of the *Kyrie* in Greek or in English, let us always implore devoutly of Christ the Lord that he will indeed shower us with his divine mercy, especially as we prepare to receive Him in Holy Mass.

6. Gloria

Next, we moved to the *center of the foyer* (location 6), and there was the famous singer by the name of Gloria, some Gloria you know personally (yourself, I suppose, if your name is Gloria) or, if all else failed, the U.S. flag—Old Glory. Gloria, of course, is a very straightforward reminder of the ancient and glorious prayer that comes next, the *Gloria,* of course:

Glory to God in the highest,
and on earth peace to people of good will.
We praise you,
we bless you,
we adore you, we glorify you,
we give you thanks for your great glory,

12 As summarized in Kevin Vost, *St. Albert the Great: Champion of Faith and Reason* (Charlotte, NC: TAN Books, 2011), 140-141.

Lord God, heavenly King,
O God, almighty Father,
Lord Jesus Christ, Only Begotten Son,
Lord God, Lamb of God, Son of the Father,
you take away the sins of the world,
have mercy on us;
you take away the sins of the world,
receive our prayer;
you are seated at the right hand of the Father,
have mercy on us.
For you alone are the Holy One,
you alone are the Lord,
you alone are the Most High,
Jesus Christ,
with the Holy Spirit,
in the glory of God the Father.
Amen.

As we move from the penitential rite to the *Gloria,* our focus moves from our own sinfulness and unworthiness to the majesty of God who so graciously cleanses our sins and so generously showers graces upon us. We echo the angels rejoicing at Christ's birth with the first line of this prayer: "Glory to God in the highest and peace on earth to those on whom his favor rests" (Luke 2:14). Indeed, it first appeared at the nighttime Christmas Mass around AD 128, when Pope St. Telesphorus proclaimed: "At the opening of the sacrifice the angelic hymn should be repeated – that is, 'Glory to God in the highest!'"[13]

Since the *Gloria* is a joyous song of praise, it is omitted during the seasons of Advent and Lent, because in Advent we await Christ's coming,

13 Cited in Cardinal Donald Wuerl and Mike Aquilina, *The Mass: The Glory, The Mystery, The Tradition* (New York: Image, 2013), 106-107.

and in Lent we meditate upon Christ's sufferings as we await his Passion and Resurrection. During most Sundays of the year though, we recite this glorious prayer in praise and gratitude to God, reciting a litany of his titles and attributes as declared in the Scriptures—as Lord and King, and also as Father, Son, and Holy Spirit, paying tribute to the mystery of the Holy Trinity. The middle lines briefly recapitulate the story of Jesus Christ, the eternally begotten Son who came into the world to offer himself as the Lamb of God to expiate our sins, and who sits eternally at the right hand of God the Father. The next time we say this prayer, let us linger on the meaning of every single word, thanking and praising God with every syllable of our speech and with every fiber of our being.

7. Collect

Next, we looked above our heads, and up in the chandelier (location 7) was a collection basket brimming over not with money but with prayers. This is because it is not time yet to actually pass around the collection basket, but it is time for the communal prayer known as the *Collect* or Opening Prayer. Though we have already prayed several prayers, in this prayer all of the prayers prayed so far are collected, so to speak, and presented to God. The priest invites us to pray silently and then proclaims aloud a prayer that announces the theme of the Mass and asks for God's intercession.

The *Collect* prayer has four main parts. The first part calls upon God the Father or the Son; the second part recalls one of God's great deeds; the third part makes a request of God; and the fourth part declares that the prayer is made through Christ's mediation.

For example, today at Mass, the twenty-fourth Sunday in Ordinary Time, readings included James 2:14-18 in which we find those most memorable words that "faith of itself, if it does not have works, is dead" (Jas 2:17) and the Gospel of St. Mark in which Jesus declares, "Whoever wishes to come after me must deny himself, take up his cross, and follow me" (Mark 8:34). Here we find the integrated Catholic (and scriptural) teaching of the roles of both faith and works, of proclaiming Christ and actually taking on his yoke. This was today's *Collect:*

> Look upon us, O God,
> Creator and ruler of all things,
> and, that we may feel the working of your mercy,
> grant that we may serve you with all our heart.
> Through our Lord Jesus Christ, your Son,
> who lives and reigns with you in the unity of the Holy Spirit,
> one God, for ever and ever.
> Amen.

I wonder, how many of our brothers and sisters in Christ who sit at Mass every week without benefit of a missal booklet even realize that the *Collect* varies at each Mass? Well, now we can be sure at least that we will not be included in that number! The *Collect* is the first of eight parts of the Mass that vary each Mass depending on the date, the liturgical season, and the particular saint or other feast of the day.[14] These prayers and readings are called the "propers" of the Mass from the Latin *proprium.* They vary and are appropriate for each occasion. The fixed parts of the Mass are called the "ordinary" parts, and they remain the same for most Masses. For the *Collect,* as for every prayer of the Mass, let us truly open our ears and our hearts so that we might heed every word, take them to heart, and go out and express our faith through the fruits of our works.

14 The propers are the Collect, first reading, responsorial psalm, second reading, Gospel acclamation, Gospel reading, Prayer over the Offerings, and the Prayer after Communion.

Repetitio Est Mater Memoriae[15]

Though we have taken several pages and several minutes in this chapter to memorize and seek a deeper understanding of the introductory rites of the Mass, note well that in real Masses they may all transpire at a rapid-fire pace. Indeed, when I last glanced down at my watch during Mass this morning at seven minutes in, these rites had all been performed and we were ready to experience the Liturgy of the Word, the subject matter of our very next chapter.

Before we move on in this book though, please note that a hallmark of true memorization is the passage of material from the fleeting capacities of short-term memory into the almost limitless stores of our long term memories. Long-term storage is demonstrated when one can recall material after a significant delay. It has probably been at least seven minutes now since we entered the memory house and encountered the first seven locations and images housed within the foyer. Recall then, if you will, those first seven locations, their images, and the parts of the Mass that they represent. Do you have them all? If yes, good show! And can you name them backward, from 7 back to 1? If not, then rehearse them again and give them another go. When you've got them all down, rehearse them again the next time you are getting ready to go to Mass. Linger on the words of each prayer as well, and with focused attention and weekly or daily repetition, eventually they too will be written on the tablet of your heart.

15 Repetition is the mother of memory.

Liturgy of the Word

"In the beginning was the Word,
and the Word was with God,
and the Word was God."
John 1:1

From the Foyer to the Living Room of the Living Word

The Bible is the "word of God," a collection of holy writings inspired by God. Its "table of contents," so to speak, for both the Old and New Testaments, was established in the fourth century by the Catholic Church under the guidance of God's Holy Spirit, when it determined which of many possible holy books were truly the inspired word of God and proclaimed the legitimate canon of Scripture. We should recall as well though, that the "word of God" itself proclaims that the Word of God with a capital "W" is Jesus Christ Himself, the Word of God incarnate. In the Liturgy of the Word at Mass, we read and hear the word of God as we celebrate the holy sacrifice of the Word of God Himself. We will return to the familiar foyer of our memory house as we begin to write the nine rites or parts of the Liturgy of the Word upon the tablets of our own hearts.

In our last chapter on the introductory rites, location 7 left us up in the chandelier with the collection basket that represented the *collect*, that is, the Opening Prayer. Now we turn our attention to location 8, a mirror hanging on the foyer's other wall, opposite the gun rack (location 5) that featured those *Valkyries* chanting the *Kyrie*. What you see in the mirror is *your own first-grade reading book.* Don't remember back that far? That will pose no problem, since you can just imagine one, maybe that classic book about Dick and Jane, or perhaps a selection from the good Dr. Seuss (just imagine whichever one you prefer and we'll put it to good use).

Under that mirror on the wall is a small cushioned bench (location 9), and seated upon that cushion is *a very talkative palm tree,* for no matter what you say to it, it instantly *responds.*

Within the cushioned bench there are some little drawers (location 10), and when you open them, what do you find but your *second-grade reader* (the book choice again is up to you, just ask yourself what Dr. Seuss might do).

Got the first-grade reader, the responsive palm, and the second reader now in the palm of your mind's hand? Sure you do. Now it's time to enter the living room to see how it is decorated with what in due course we'll reveal to you as the next parts of the Liturgy of the Word.

Our eleventh location is the center of the living room, and here you see a young street corner newsboy from days gone by, a satchel around his neck full of newspapers, holding one in his hand as he shouts to you, "*Good news! Good news!* Come and get it!" Location 12 is what you see in the backyard as you gaze out the living room's big picture window, and there is that newsboy again, and you wonder what he is up to as he drenches his *Good Newspaper* in a vat of wet ink and uses the dripping ink to *dye a log* that sits under it. (This one might take a little explaining, so stay tuned for the next section.)

Gazing back within the living room and turning a bit to your right, you see that sitting upon the sofa (14) is that same newsboy again resting and *reading* one of his *Good Newspapers*. Now in front of the couch is a great big coffee table (15), but what sits on it is not coffee but a piping hot bowl full of *hominy grits.* (That makes my mouth water. I don't know about you!) On the other side of that table on the wall with the picture window is a big-screen TV (15) and on it is a most unusual interview show, for there is your own favorite TV host interviewing three unusual women in ancient Greek attire. They *profess* that they are three fabled *fates* as they all sit there spinning thread.

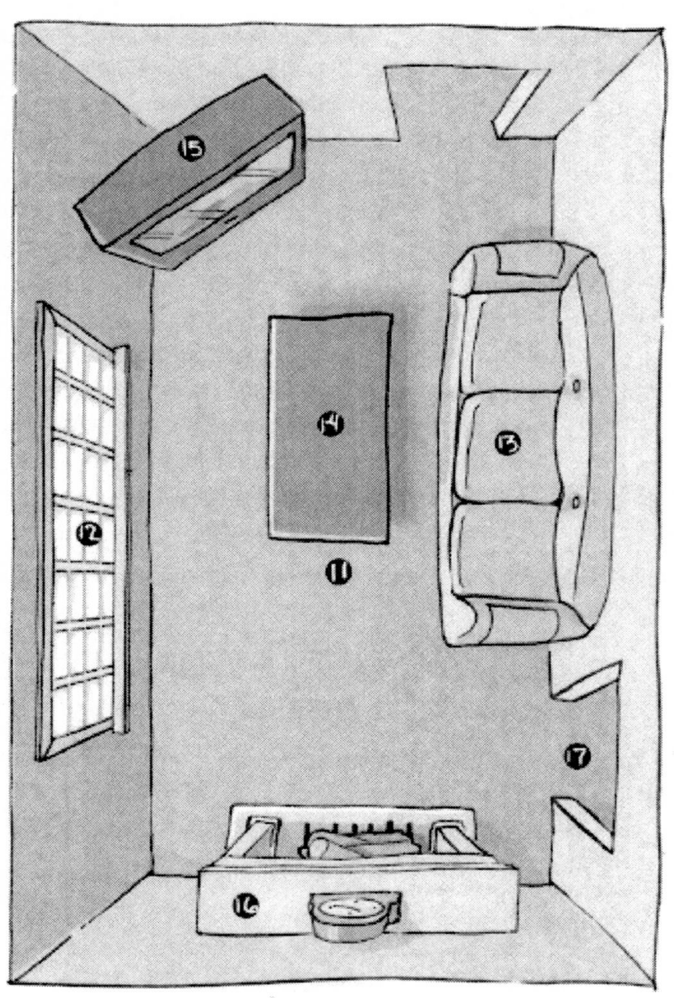

The Living Room

Indeed, they then all stand up and tell the host that they are *"professional fates."* Finally (for this chapter anyway), you peer across that room at the fireplace (16) and see not logs and flames but a reflection from the view out the top of the chimney—a reflection of a vast and *starry universe*—but most strangely of all you see the Big Dipper itself clasped within two gigantic *hands* that then fold themselves *in prayer.*

Whew! Do you have now the first reader in the mirror (8), the responsive palm tree on the cushioned bench (9), the second reader in the drawer (10), the newsboy acclaiming "Good news!" in the center of the living room (11), dying a log in the backyard (12), reading his *Good Newspaper* on the sofa (13), near which sits the hominy grits on the coffee table (14), not far from the professional fates on the TV (15), and across the room from that fireplace that held the universe, which in its turn was held within hands of prayer (16)? If you do, Bravo! If not, please go over them a time or two, and if the mood hits you, see if you can name them all in reverse, from 16 back to 8. So, once you got them all down, let's proceed to see just how holy and valuable are the things that those images help us recall.

LOCATION	***IMAGE***	**PART OF THE MASS**
8. Mirror	*First-grade reader*	First reading
9. Bench	*Responsive palm tree*	Responsorial psalm
10. Drawer	*Second-grade reader*	Second reading
11. Center of living room	*Newsboy acclaims "Good news!"*	Gospel acclamation
12. Picture window	*Newsboy dyes a log*	Gospel dialogue
13. Sofa	*Newsboy reads Good Newspaper*	Gospel reading

14. Coffee table	*Hominy*	Homily
15. Big-screen TV	*Professional fates*	Profession of Faith
16. Fireplace	*Universe within praying hands*	Universal Prayer

If you have perused the table, do these images begin to make sense now? Anybody have any "Ahas!"? Well, as far as our memory work goes, note well that we are nearly half done already with the parts of the *Novus Ordo* Mass! Our work is also only half done for this chapter though, since we need to dig in to better understand the nature of these nine parts of the Liturgy of the Word so that when you recall these images, you'll also recall and revere the sacred rites they represent.

8. First Reading

That first-grade reader in the mirror (location 8) signifies for us that the introductory rites have been completed, and now we stand ready (*sit* actually!) to hear the words of Scripture. In the earliest description we have of the Mass, in a letter to the Roman Emperor Antoninus Pius in the second century AD, St. Justin Martyr wrote that on Sunday, when Christians were gathered together in the same place, "the memoirs of the apostles and the writings of the prophets are read, as much as time permits."[1] The early Christians knew well, as St. Paul had informed them, that "faith comes from what is heard" (Rom 10:17). So then, for more than nineteen hundred years at least, Christians have heard readings at Mass before the Eucharist. Justin noted that the readings came from the writings of the prophets and the apostles, and to this day the first reading comes usually from the texts of the Old Testament, but also from the Acts of the Apostles during the Easter Season. Christ said he came not to abolish the law and prophets but to fulfill them (see Matt 5:17). When St. Paul wrote to

1 St. Justin, *Apology,* 1, 65, as cited in the *Catechism of the Catholic Church*, 2nd ed. (New York: Doubleday, 2003), 1345.

Timothy that all Scripture is inspired by God and profitable for teaching (see 2 Tim 3:16), the Scriptures he referred to were indeed the writings we now call the Old Testament, since the New Testament books had yet to be written and canonized as the twenty-seven books we know today. As the *Catechism of the Catholic Church* makes crystal clear, "The Old Testament is an indispensable part of Sacred Scripture. Its books are divinely inspired and retain a permanent value, for the Old Covenant has never been revoked" (121).

So then, we now sit and listen as a reader (*lector* in Latin) stands behind a pulpit (*lectern* in Latin or *ambo* in Greek) from a book of readings called the *lectionary*. It contains the readings as they appear in Scripture, but it sometimes alters a word here or there to make the readings understandable because only brief passages are used. For example, if a reading of several verses started with the word "he" or "they," the lectionary would spell out the person's or group's name rather than starting with an undefined pronoun. Before he reads the passage, the lector proclaims, "A reading from the book of (name of the particular book)," and at the end the lector proclaims, "The Word of the Lord," and we respond, "Thanks be to God."

By hearing the first readings at Mass, Catholics absorb a great deal of the Scriptures as the years roll by in the three-year cycle of readings. Attentive Mass-goers who would participate fully are also advised to note that the theme or events of the first reading will in some way set the stage and prepare the way to that day's Gospel reading four memory images down the road (or in the living room for us).

Staying with the example of the twenty-fourth Sunday in Ordinary Time, our first reading was from the book of Isaiah 50:5-9a. It opens as follows: "The Lord GOD opens my ear that I may hear; and I have not rebelled, have not turned back. I gave my back to those who beat me, my cheeks to those who plucked my beard; my face I did not shield from buffets and spitting." It reminds us most clearly and graphically that we are called to take up our crosses and follow Christ, whatever might befall us. It reminds us as well of the assistance that will be provided us: "See, the Lord GOD is my help; who will prove me wrong?"

9. Responsorial Psalm

Below the mirror on the cushioned bench (location 9) was that responsive palm tree, serving so well to remind us of the responsorial psalm. While we remain seated a reader or singer (*cantor* in Latin) provides one verse, usually from the Psalms, to which we respond out loud by repeating it. This repeated verse is called the *antiphon,* from Greek, meaning "returning sound." The lector or cantor then reads or sings additional verses, holds out his or her hand to signal us when it's our turn, and we again respond with the same verse.[2] To continue with the Mass of the twenty-fourth Sunday in Ordinary Time in the year 2015 as our example, here is the beginning and first of four refrains of the responsorial psalm from Psalm 116:

> Cantor: I will walk before the Lord, in the land of the living. I love the LORD because he has heard my voice in supplication, because he has inclined his ear to me the day I called.
>
> People: I will walk before the Lord, in the land of the living.

A missal or guidebook to the Mass may include the musical notation for the repeating verse or antiphon of the Psalm, and whether it does or not, the Psalm, if sung, will first be sung by the cantor. The Psalms themselves have been greatly venerated throughout the history of the Catholic Church, partly because they are cited more often than any other book of the Old Testament within the books of the New Testament. They are great works of praise and prayer that address almost all human feelings and circumstances from the deepest of suffering to the greatest heights of joy. Church Fathers noted too that these psalms or prayers of King David anticipated Christ, were addressed to Christ, and indeed were in a sense, Christ's own prayers.[3] In early medieval times, the Benedictine Rule of St. Ferreolus of Uzes (AD 530-581) noted that "anyone who wishes to be

2 To quote a popular song from some decades ago, "Second verse, same as the first!"

3 See Michael Dubruiel's *The How-to-Book of the Mass* (Huntington, IN: Our Sunday Visitor, 2007) for a brief, but helpful look at the way that the Psalms reference Christ.

worthy of the name of monk" must hold all 150 of the Psalms in his memory, "in their entirety!"[4] Thankfully for us, at Mass we're merely expected to recall and repeat but one verse at a time!

At rare special times another scriptural canticle, such as Mary's *Magnificat* prayer (Luke 1:46-55), will be used in the place of a Psalm. In any case, the responsorial psalm gives us a chance to pray together to God together with Christ – or with his Holy Mother!

10. Second Reading

Next in our memory tour was the drawer in the small cushioned bench (location 10) in which we found our second-grade reader to remind us of the second reading. Now, during weekend Masses, the lector reads a passage from one of the New Testament letters or *epistles (*from the Greek, meaning "something sent"), most often those of St. Paul, from the Acts of the Apostles, or from Revelation. This is most fitting since many of these letters were indeed originally intended to be read aloud by early Christian congregations while they celebrated Mass![5] Here, now, at every Sunday Mass two millennia down the road, we too are instructed by the words of the apostles themselves in what it means to live as a member of the body of Christ. As was the case with the first reading, before he reads the passage, the lector proclaims, "A reading from the book of (name of the particular book)." At the end the lector proclaims, "The Word of the Lord," and we respond, "Thanks be to God."

Our second reading for the twenty-fourth Sunday in Ordinary Time was from the book of St. James 2:14-18. Emphasizing again the theme that Christ has asked us not merely to acknowledge his name but also to follow him in every act of our lives, it includes these powerful words:

> If a brother or sister has nothing to wear and has no food for the day, and one of you says to them, 'Go in peace, keep warm, and eat well,' but you do not give them the necessities of the body, what good is it? So also faith of itself, if it does not have works, is dead.

4 Carruthers, *The Book of Memory*, 88.

5 Refer, for examples, to 1 Thessalonians 5:27 and Revelation 1:3.

At this point it is up to us how deeply we will participate in the Liturgy of the Word. Will we choose to pay close attention to these words and to put them into practice in our daily lives? When we exit the church's doors today, will we carry on as if the Mass did not happen, or will we choose to enliven our faith with real works of loving charity toward our brothers and sisters in Christ?

11. Gospel Acclamation

Here, in the center of the living room (11) we saw that good newsboy proclaiming good news, the best news of all news, in fact, for now we are moving from the words of Christ's apostles to the words of Christ himself contained within the Gospels. "Good news" is the modern English translation of the Old English Word "gospel," translated from the original Greek word *evangelion.*[6] We stand at this point, to honor Christ's words and deeds which we are about to hear.

If we would listen to the words our good newsboy calls out first, they would actually be neither new nor old English, nor Greek, but Hebrew in fact (or a Latinized version thereof)! The newsboy represents the priest

6 That the news of Christ has long been acclaimed as the good news, we can look, for example, to Acts 8:35: "Then Philip opened his mouth, and beginning with this scripture he told him the good news of Jesus…"

or the deacon, and what he acclaims is "Alleluia!" (the Latinized form of the Hebrew *Hallelujah*), which means "praise the Lord" (more literally "praise Yahweh"). We find these words of pure praise to God in several of the Psalms (113-118) that the Hebrews called *Hallel* or "Praise Psalms," and we see the Alleluia repeated four times in the great marriage supper of the Lamb in the first six verses of Revelation (or Apocalypse) chapter 19.

Let's take a minute now to contemplate the fact that we at Sunday Mass,[7] perhaps at our little parish church right down the street, join in with the ancient Hebrews and with the choirs of angels and saints in heaven as well, when we too sing out or chant "Alleluia!" praising God as we prepare to receive the good news He is about to share with us.

12. Gospel Dialogue

Here, peering through the picture window (12) into the backyard, we saw our good newsboy dying a log with newspaper ink. Now why would he "dye a log" if not to remind us of the Gospel dialogue? Though lay lectors and cantors may proclaim the earlier readings, only a priest or deacon proclaims the Gospel. If the priest proclaims it, he recites a silent prayer that God will cleanse his heart and lips. If a deacon is to proclaim it, then the priest or bishop blesses him with this prayer:

May the Lord be in your heart and on your lips,
that you may proclaim his Gospel worthily and well,
in the name of the Father, and of the Son, and of
the Holy Spirit.

The deacon responds: Amen.

In beseeching God's assistance in proclaiming the Gospel well, even this brief rite of dialogue makes clear how the Church recognizes what a

7 The Alleluia is not proclaimed during Lent as we prepare for Christ's Passion and await the Easter season of the most joyful praise to God. One of eight other invocations are used instead during Lent, such as the first: *"Glory and praise to you, Lord Jesus Christ!"*

glorious thing and great gift to us is the Gospel of Jesus Christ.

13. Gospel Reading

Now we are back inside and arriving at the living room sofa (13), and we see our good newsboy reading his good newspaper. In the reality that is the Mass, our sofa represents the pulpit, our newsboy represents the priest or the deacon, and the good news he's reading is the Gospel of our Lord Jesus Christ. Still standing now, the priest or deacon proclaims, "The Lord be with you," and we the people respond, "And with your spirit." He then declares, "A reading from the Holy Gospel according to (name of one of the four Gospel evangelists)," while making the sign of three small crosses over the forehead, lips, and heart. We do the same and respond, "Glory to you, O Lord."

The deacon proclaims, "The Gospel of the Lord," to which we respond, "Praise to you, Lord Jesus Christ." The crossing gestures symbolize our willingness to open our minds to the words of the Gospel, to proclaim it with our lips, and to engrave it in our hearts.

As we stand, we listen to a passage from several verses to a page or two long from one of the four Gospels laid out in the Church's three-year cycle in which we hear from all four evangelists, Sts. Matthew, Mark, Luke, and John. Here, week (or day) after week (or day) and year after year, we are blessed to hear of the words and the deeds of God, which the Word Himself willingly made flesh in the Lord Jesus Christ, so that we might be saved and enjoy eternal life with him. Well, what shall we do now? Will we yawn through His story, perhaps thinking about lunch or the afternoon's activities, or shall we stand there in awe, lifting up our hearts and minds to thank Christ for what he has done for us, ready to absorb his lessons, so that we might become more like Him?

You'll recall the coordination of themes in the readings of the various parts of the Mass. In keeping with the example of the twenty-fourth Sunday in Ordinary Time, which it was when I started writing this book, our Gospel reading was Mark 8:27-35. Here, in this most memorable passage, Jesus asks his disciples who they thought he was. Peter answers him rightly, "You are the Christ."

Christ then starts to describe the suffering he must endure, even unto his death. Peter then rebukes Christ for saying such things must happen, and Christ responds to him, "Get thee behind me, Satan. You are thinking not as God does, but as human beings do." Humans tend to try to avoid suffering at all costs. Look at an extreme example today of the push for legalized euthanasia, "mercy killing," and "physician-assisted suicide." God knows there can be merit in suffering, and even if we are not to be called on to endure great suffering, let alone martyrdom, to follow Christ is to open ourselves to such possibilities, as well as to the certainty that we will all encounter crosses of some kind that we must bear. As Christ Himself concludes:

> Whoever wishes to come after me must deny himself, take up his cross, and follow me. For whoever wishes to save his life will lose it, but whoever loses his life for my sake and that of the gospel will save it.

Being a Christian is sometimes no easy thing, and the signs of our times make clear it is becoming even less easy, as laws are enacted that run counter to our faith, putting citizenship and conscience at odds. On a smaller, more personal level, perhaps even the discipline of memorizing the Mass is like a small cross to some! We must remember as well though that the same Christ who calls us to take up his cross gladly helps us shoulder the load. He has openly promised his loving support: "for I am gentle and lowly in heart, and you will find rest for your souls. For my yoke is easy, and my burden is light" (Matt 11:29-30).

Have we prayed to Christ then, to help us stand up for our faith no matter what, and to help us memorize the Mass, so that we might know it and love it more deeply as the greatest of all prayers to Him (and through Him and with Him as well)?

14. Homily

On the coffee table (14) in front of the sofa was a piping hot bowl of hominy, that delicious Southern dish, sitting there to remind us that now it is our turn to sit and enjoy the nourishment of this Sunday's homily, delivered by the priest or deacon. The word "homily" comes from the Greek *homilia* for "a discourse with another person or persons." Quite fittingly, the word is used in Luke 24:13-14 when the two apostles on the road to Emmaus were talking and discussing the events of Christ's Crucifixion with each other, when Christ himself appeared to them in his glorified body. They did not recognize him until after he had broken bread, and he then proceeded to open up the Scriptures to them (Luke 24:32). The reference is most fitting because the very purpose of a homily is to open up the Scriptures to the people at Mass.

As we sit to hear the homily, the priest, in the person of Christ and guided by the Holy Spirit, strives to open the meaning of the day's Gospel reading to us, to impart a catechetical message, and to inspire us to carry forth that Gospel message out into our lives for the rest of the week. So again we have a choice to make. Are we going to let our minds wander, deciding perhaps, we don't care for this priest's or deacon's speaking style since it doesn't "move" or "feed" us (meaning really perhaps that it does not "entertain" us), or are we going to open up our own hearts to receive some message that God may have in mind for us today? Will we keep our ears and minds focused so that we do not miss it? And if we do catch that message, will we be willing to memorize it, to engrave it on the tablets of our hearts, and to live it out in our lives? The message is the Holy Spirit's. The decision of whether or not to hear and heed it is ours.

15. Profession of Faith

Next in our mnemonic tour were those "professional fates" upon the screen of the big-screen television (15). Those professional fates were merely there to remind us of the Profession of Faith. After the homily and a moment or two of silent reflection, the priest and the people rise to profess before God and each other those essential tenets of the faith that have brought them together at Mass, starting with the words, "I believe..." Here, each one of us personally declares essential beliefs about God as one substance; God as three persons in the Trinity; the Father as the Creator; Jesus Christ as God made incarnate of the Holy Virgin through the workings of the Holy Spirit; Christ's Crucifixion, Death, Resurrection, Ascension, and his Coming Judgment; and one, holy, catholic, and apostolic Church that we share in through one Baptism so that our sins may be forgiven and so that we too may be resurrected and share in eternal life.[8]

The words we recited are those of the Nicene Creed. More detailed than the briefer Apostle's Creed, it grew out of Church Councils at Nicaea in AD 325 and Constantinople in 381. The creed came to include more essential details in response to various heresies that distorted the faith by denying the full divinity of Christ and of the Holy Spirit. The Nicene Creed (and we with it) proclaims that Christ is not merely a man or a creature of God, but God, *consubstantial,* of one substance with the Father, and that the Holy Spirit is "the Lord, the giver of life, who proceeds from the Father and the Son, who with the Father and the Son is adored and glorified, who has spoken through the prophets…" See any missal or other sources for the words of the Creed itself, and say it again at Mass and after Mass, until its very words have been written in your heart. And be aware as well, that every word in the Creed is pregnant with profound meaning. Indeed, part one of the four parts of the *Catechism of the Catholic Church* is dedicated to expounding the Creed,[9] running from pages 17-299! So do make some time when you can, to prayerfully read that first part of the *Catechism*, so when you proclaim "I believe" you'll more fully understand just what you're proclaiming.

16. Universal Prayer

We moved along next to the fireplace (16) where we saw a starry universe and two massive hands, larger than galaxies, folded together in

---

8 I direct you to *The Roman Missal*, pp. 723-725 for the exact words of the Nicene Creed and 725-727 for the Apostle's Creed.

9 Part I is "The Profession of Faith." Part II is "The Celebration of the Christian Mystery" (focusing on the liturgy and sacraments). Part III is "Life in Christ" (focusing on Christian living and addressing topics including the beatitudes, conscience, virtues, social justice, and natural law). Part IV is "Christian Prayer" (focusing on a detailed exposition of the Lord's Prayer, which "in the Eucharistic liturgy the Lord's Prayer appears as the prayer of the whole Church and there reveals its full meaning and efficacy." *CCC*, 2770).

prayer. This scene should call to our minds the next part of the Mass, the Universal Prayer, also known as the Prayer of the Faithful. Now the lector or cantor invokes a series of supplications or petitions to God for the needs of the Church, our nation, and the entire world, for any people in need, and for the needs of the local parish and community. After each petition, the people respond, "Lord, hear our prayer," inspired by Psalm 130:2: "Lord, hear my cry! May your ears be attentive to my cry for mercy."

With our communal petitions to God, the Liturgy of the Word is closed and the glorious, mysterious Liturgy of the Eucharist is about to begin. Before we begin in our next chapter, let's take some time to review and rehearse. Have you memorized all sixteen parts of the Mass so far: 1) entrance song, 2) greeting, 3) sprinkling of holy water, 4) penitential rite, 5) *Kyrie*, 6) *Gloria*, 7) Collect, 8) first reading, 9) responsorial psalm, 10) second reading, 11) Gospel acclamation, 12) Gospel dialogue, 13) Gospel, 14) homily, 15) Profession of Faith, and 16) Universal Prayer? If not, please review the mnemonic tours and illustrations of chapters one and two once more (or peek ahead to Appendix A and study the master table).

Next we will move to the holiest of all tables, the altar table of the holy sacrifice of the Mass.

Liturgy of the Eucharist

The Eucharist is the heart and the summit of the Church's life…
Catechism of the Catholic Church (1407)

Preparing to Dine Through, With, and On with Christ

The Eucharist is far more than any simple meal, of course, but at this point in our memory house we prepare to enter the dining room which will indeed house the Lord's Supper, the holy sacrifice and sacrament of the Eucharist in which Christ himself becomes truly present to us and presents to us the bread of life.

Join me then at location 17, the living room doorway that leads into the dining room. Here you find a large stack of *gift-wrapped presents,* and your heart leaps with joy as if you were a child on Christmas morning (which, in a sense, at this point in the Mass, we are, as children of God awaiting Christ's appearance). You take a step across the threshold and there at the adjoining *dining room doorway* (18), you spy a large, golden, *engraved invitation*. It is addressed to you, and on the cover it pictures a beautifully vested priest holding up and out his hands in prayer in the ancient *orans* posture imitating Christ on the cross. Moving along to the chair at the head of the dining room table (19), you find *your own parish priest praying over those gift-wrapped presents*. Smack dab in the center of the table (20), your mouth waters as you find a great, golden *Thanksgiving turkey,* sitting there for a great family feast.

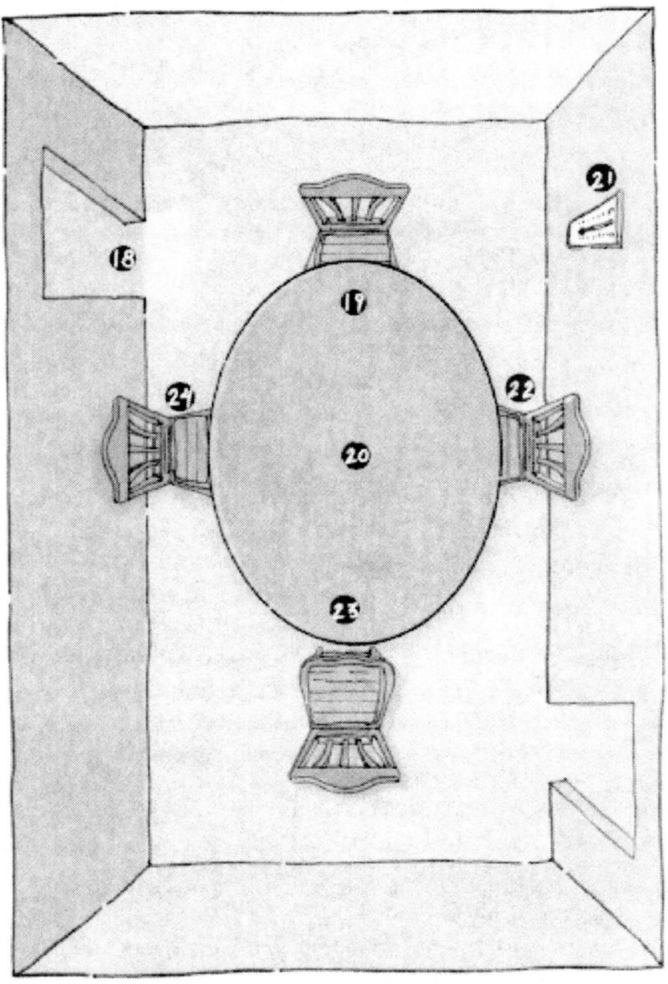

The Dining Room

Now, up on the wall next to the table is a large *wall thermometer* (21). The thermometer has been carved from a log, and for some reason yet unknown, there you see the face of your parish priest, and he, like that newsboy out in the backyard, is dyeing that log for some reason (in red and in black, to be exact)![1] Back now to the dining room table, and at the first seat on the left (22), you see your *priest's face* again. At the chair at the foot of the table (23), there is your *priest's face* again, except this time you hear him as well, for he's making a loud *acclamation.*

That was our last stop in our memory tour for this chapter, but we are not quite finished yet, for now, with our mind's eyes, we must zoom in on the priest at the head of the table, for this is a location of such crucial importance that we need to elaborate with several additional images, five more to be exact.

Still at the head of the table, you notice that next to the priest's face, whispering into his right ear is a beautiful, *pure white dove*. The priest then raises his arms and you see he is holding a *host* with the image of a *crucifix* emblazoned upon it. Next to the priest is a surprising sight: a beautiful, statuesque ancient Greek goddess, *Mnemosyne* to be exact, the Greek patron saint (actually, goddess) of *memory!*[2] Next to *Mnemosyne* stands a real and even more beautiful woman, the *Blessed Virgin Mary*, surrounded by the *apostles* and legions of holy *saints.* Last, but not least, you notice that kneeling next to one of the saints (St. Dominic perhaps)[3] is the biggest

---

1 In sacred texts, the words to be spoken have traditionally been written in black ink, while instructions on what is to be done are written in red ink. These guiding comments are called "rubrics" from the Latin word for red.

2 *Mnemosyne,* or Memory, was said to be the "Mother of the Muses," the mother of nine goddesses representing epic poetry, history, music, lyric poetry, tragedy, hymns, dance, comedy, and astronomy, since all depend upon memory for their perfection. Her name is carried on in our words *mnemonic* and *mnemonics* as an adjective referring to memory aiding effects or a noun referring to the memory aids themselves. In this book we use mnemonic techniques which themselves can be called mnemonics.

3 Shortly before his birth, Dominic's mother, Blessed Juana of Aza, received a vision in which she gave birth to a dog bearing a torch that would go forth to enlighten the world.

dachshund that you have ever seen. All right then, it is time to review and rehearse all of these scenes using this summary chart:

LOCATION	*IMAGE(S)*	PART OF MASS
17. Living room doorway	*Gift-wrapped presents*	Presentation of Gifts
18. Dining room doorway	*Engraved invitation*	Invitation to Prayer
19. Foot of table	*Your priest prays over presents*	Prayer over the Offerings
20. Center of table	*Thanksgiving turkey dinner*	Eucharistic Prayer
21. Thermometer	*Face of priest/ dyes a log*	Preface Dialogue
22. Seat on right	*Your priest's face*	Preface
23. Head of table	*Your priest's face proclaiming*	Preface Acclamation
	Dove whispers into his ear	Epiclesis
	He holds host with crucifix	Institution/Consecration
	Mnemosyne next to him	Anamnesis
	Blessed Mary and saints	Intercessions
	Huge dachshund	Great Doxology

17. Presentation and Preparation of the Gifts

The gift-wrapped presents at the living room doorway (17) represent the gifts that we offer at Mass in this first rite of the Liturgy of the Eucharist. In the early days of the Church, Christians presented at the altar bread or wine or various fruits of their labors, including actual fruits, like figs, grapes, pomegranates, apples, etc., and sometimes fresh flowers too. Monetary gifts were given too, as St. Paul wrote about (1 Cor 16: 1-4), and as they are in our day.[4] Our monetary gifts cover the considerable costs involved in maintaining the Church, and some will also be dispensed for the needs of the poor. Let's reflect a bit then upon our own offering. Are we showing gratitude and generosity for a Church that has given so much to us in our life on earth and our journey toward heaven?

So, at this point in Mass, while the collection is taken up in the nave of the church, and while the people sing an offertory song, upon the altar the priest, altar servers, and deacon, if present, prepare the altar for the great Eucharistic sacrifice. The Liturgy of the Word was based at the lectern or ambo, while the Liturgy of the Eucharist transpires upon the altar. Upon it are arranged the *paten* or plate that holds the bread to be consecrated; the *chalice* that holds the water and wine that will also soon be consecrated; the *corporal,* the square linen cloth upon which the paten and chalice sit; along with the *purificator,* another linen cloth used to clean the chalice; and finally the *missal* (formerly known as the *sacramentary*), the book containing the prayers of the Mass.

After the altar has been prepared and the gifts have been received, the priest prepares the elements of the bread, water, and wine. The priest then prays in a low voice:[5]

> Blessed are you, Lord God of all creation, for through your goodness we have received the bread we offer you: fruit of the earth and work of human hands, it will become for us the bread of life.

4 The fifth of five "Precepts of the Church" that establish bare minimums for active Church membership and spiritual growth is to provide for the material needs of the Church, according to one's abilities. The first four address Mass attendance on Sundays and Holy Days, at least once yearly confession, at least once yearly reception of the Eucharist during the Easter season, and observation of fasting and abstinence on days established by the Church. (See *CCC*, 2041 and 2042).

5 He may also say this prayer aloud if the offertory song is sung.

The people respond: Blessed be God for ever.

The priest or deacon then pours wine and a small amount of water into the chalice, praying inaudibly:

By the mystery of this water and wine may we come to share in the divinity of Christ who humbled himself to share in our humanity.

Before returning the chalice to the altar, he says:

Blessed are you, Lord God of all creation, for through your goodness we have received the wine we offer you: fruit of the vine and work of human hands, it will become our spiritual drink.

People: Blessed be God for ever.

The priest then prays inaudibly:

With humble spirit and contrite heart may we be accepted by you, O Lord, and may our sacrifice in your sight this day be pleasing to you, Lord God.

The priest then washes his hands,[6] saying:

Wash me, O Lord, from my iniquity and cleanse me from my sin.

Now, with clean hands and pure hearts, everything is in place for our priest to call us to prayer.

---

6 We will examine the history and significance of this hand-washing ritual in our examination of the *Lavabo* in Part II on the Latin Mass.

18. Invitation to Prayer

Our first step into the mnemonic dining room where we soon will dine with Christ lands us just inside the doorway (18), where we found a large invitation engraved in gold with our own name. This golden invitation represents the priest's invitation to us to join him in prayer about the holy sacrifice so soon to take place.

The priest says out loud:

Pray, brethren (brothers and sisters), that my sacrifice and Yours may be acceptable to God, the almighty Father.

The people then stand and respond:

May the Lord accept the sacrifice at your hands, for the praise and glory of his name, for our good and the good of all his holy Church.

19. Prayer Over the Offerings

Our next stop in the dining room was at a chair at the foot of the dining room table (19), and we saw your own priest praying over the gift-wrapped presents, which have been unwrapped, revealing bread and wine. This is a pretty straightforward representation of the Prayer over the Offerings or Gifts. This prayer is one of the propers that change with each Mass. Persisting in our original example of the twenty-fourth Sunday in Ordinary Time, this is the prayer that is proper for the priest to pray today:

Look with favor on our supplications, O Lord, and in your kindness accept these, your servant's offerings, that what each has offered to the honor of your name may serve the salvation of all.

The people respond: Amen.

20. Eucharistic Prayer

Sitting upon the dining room table (20) we saw that enormous Thanksgiving turkey. That turkey represents for us commencement of the greatest of all thanksgivings, the prayers that prepare for the *Eucharist* (literally "thanksgiving" in the Greek), in which Christ gives his very self to us. The Eucharistic Prayer unfolds in a sequence that will carry us through the end of the dining room and through the end of this chapter. Let's move along then and feast on this greatest of thanksgiving prayers.

21. Preface Dialogue

At the site of the wall thermometer (21) we saw your priest's face. The thermometer was carved from a log, and for some reason, your priest was dyeing the log. The priest's face simply reminds us of the spelling and sound of the word "preface." He is dyeing a log, because the second word of interest here is, of course, dialogue. That's enough then for the reason we used such an image. Now it is time to see what it means. The Preface Dialogue begins the grand and beautiful Eucharistic Prayer that will be said by the priest alone, acting in the person of Christ. In the preface dialogue we are clearly reminded, however, that we too participate in the holy sacrifice that is about to begin.

Priest: The Lord be with you.
People: And with your spirit.

Priest: Lift up your hearts.
People: We lift them up to the Lord.
Priest: Let us give thanks to the Lord our God.
People: It is right and just.

Here, we have participated in a give-and-take dialogue with our priest that dates back to the earliest centuries of the Church. We have acknowledged God's presence in the priest and in us, lifted up our hearts to God, leaving our earthly concerns behind, and thanked God for all he has given us and for the gift of himself that he is about to give us.

22. Preface

In our memory tour we moved to the chair at the left of the dining room table (22), and there we saw your priest's smiling face again (only this time he's not dyeing a log!). The priest's face reminds us of the Preface itself. This prayer in preparation for the great Eucharistic Prayer is another proper, varying with Church season and with the nature of special Masses, for particular feasts, marriages, or funerals. Indeed, there are more than fifty of them.[7] Each of these prayers gives thanks to God with a special emphasis that fits the liturgical occasion. Eight of these prayers are for use in Ordinary Time. I'll provide as an example Ordinary Sunday Preface V, a prayer with special emphasis on thanking God for all of creation:

> It is truly right and just, our duty and our salvation, always an everywhere to Give you thanks, Lord, holy Father, almighty and eternal God. For you laid the foundations of the world and have arranged the changing of times and seasons; you formed man in your own image and set humanity over the whole world in all its wonder, to rule in your name over all you have made

7 In the *New St. Joseph's Sunday Missal*, I count fifty-four!

> and for ever praise you in your mighty works, through Christ our Lord. And so, with all the Angels, we praise you as in joyful celebration we acclaim.

What we joyfully acclaim are the words of the *Sanctus,* which we'll find at the head of the table.

23. Preface Acclamation

At the head of the table (23) we saw our priest again, and the first thing we noticed was that he was proclaiming something. What he was proclaiming (and we along with him) is the preface acclamation, also known as the *Sanctus:*

> Holy, Holy, Holy Lord God of hosts.
> Heaven and earth are full of your glory.
> Hosanna in the highest.
> Blessed is he who comes in the name of the Lord.
> Hosanna in the highest.

The "Holy, Holy, Holy" acclamation goes back to the Jewish prayers in the synagogues and echoes Isaiah 6:3: "Holy, Holy, Holy is the LORD of hosts. All the earth is filled with his glory!" We see these words of highest praise in the heavenly Mass too: "Holy, holy, holy is the Lord God almighty, who was, and who is, and who is to come" (Rev 4:8). Tradition holds the three holies glorify the Father, the Son, and the Holy Spirit. As for the Hosanna parts, Hosanna is Hebrew for "save us," and we see these words in Matthew 21:9: "Hosanna to the Son of David. Blessed is he who comes in the name of the Lord; hosanna in the highest."

You'll recall that this memory location was different from the others in that it contained not one image but six. This allows us to stay with the numbering of rites as laid out in the *St. Joseph Missal,* and it also gives us opportunity to delve a bit deeper into the Catholic art of memory by employing an additional memory method, known as "linking" or "chaining." Each of our locations can hold many more than merely one image, if additional images are related to each other in such a way that one image leads to the other. The Eucharistic Prayer is of such length, such grandeur, and such intricate arrangement that it certainly warrants our extra efforts.

So, the Preface has now been acclaimed, and we kneel as the priest begins the Eucharistic Prayer itself, choosing from several options in the missal. Recall that after the priest proclaimed the acclamation you noticed that whispering into his right ear was the purest of white doves. The dove has long been a representation of the Holy Spirit (perhaps in no small part, due to the fact that all four Gospels relate the Holy Spirit descended on Christ like a dove at the time of his Baptism). Here, the dove serves to remind us that regardless of the particular Eucharistic Prayer used, after the

Preface comes the *Epiclesis,* from the Greek that means to "invoke upon."[8] Here, for example, is the epiclesis from the brief Eucharistic Prayer 2:

> Make holy, therefore, these gifts, we pray, by sending down your Spirit upon them like the dewfall, so that they may become for us the Body and Blood of our Lord Jesus Christ.

Next in our memory tour, we saw the priest raise aloft a host with the image of a crucifix upon it. The image is not entirely odd, since hosts may be imprinted with the form of a cross, but in this image, you see in three dimensions, the crucified Christ himself upon the host. This image serves to remind us of the heart of the heart of the sacrifice of the Mass, the Institution Narrative and the Consecration in which the bread and wine, through the power of God, become the Body and Blood, soul and divinity of Jesus Christ himself.

We have just pledged to lift up our hearts to the Lord, and now the Lord himself comes down to bring his heart and his all to us. Through the power given to the priest through his ordination, he is able to stand in the person of Christ, and through the power of God, make present in what appears to our eyes as mere bread and wine, the real, sacramental presence of Christ. Here are the words of consecration from Eucharistic Prayer 2:

> At the time he was betrayed and entered willingly into his Passion, he took bread and, giving thanks, broke it, and gave it to his disciples, saying:
>
> TAKE THIS, ALL OF YOU, AND EAT OF IT, FOR THIS IS MY BODY, WHICH WILL BE GIVEN UP FOR YOU.

8 If you'd care to remember the sound and the meaning of the word *epiclesis*, I might suggest the image of the old Stoic philosopher Epictetus, complete with a holy dove whispering in his ear.

In a similar way, when supper was ended, he took the chalice and, once more giving thanks, he gave it to his disciples saying:

TAKE THIS, ALL OF YOU, AND DRINK FROM IT, FOR THIS IS THE CHALICE OF MY BLOOD,
THE BLOOD OF THE NEW AND ETERNAL COVENANT, WHICH WILL BE POURED OUT FOR YOU AND FOR MANY FOR THE FORGIVENESS OF SINS. DO THIS IN MEMORY OF ME.

These words, of course, draw from Christ's words in all of the Gospel accounts of the Last Supper, and also nearly repeat verbatim the account of St. Paul from 1 Corinthians 11:25. This is the greatest glory, gift, and mystery of the Holy Sacrifice of the Mass. Theologians have explained, to the best of their understanding, that the elements of bread and wine have been "transubstantiated." Their substance, the essence of what they truly are, has become the body and blood of Christ, as Christ himself has promised (most explicitly seen in John 6). Their "accidents," the sensible qualities we can perceive with our senses, still remain the same. We see Christ's real presence not with the eyes that rest beneath our brows, but with the eyes of faith.[9]

Moving along in our memory tour, still with our priest at the head of the table (23), we saw on his left side a somewhat surprising image, considering the situation, for there was the mythological Greek goddess *Mnemosyne,* the "Mother of the Muses." She is there to remind us of the part of the Eucharistic Prayer called the *Anamnesis,* meaning (in Greek, of course) "a reminiscence, remembrance, or recollection." Here, we recall that Christ explicitly bade us, "Do this in remembrance of me" (Luke 22:19; 1 Cor 11:24). We have heard these words above at the end of the

9 See Appendix C for a detailed explanation (and complete memory tour) of some of the reasons why the Catholic Church has always with confidence proclaimed Christ's Real Presence in the Holy Eucharist.

words of consecration, and not only have we *remembered* Christ's words and actions, we have *done* as he instructed us to do.

Next to Mnemosyne was an image far more familiar and far more beautiful still, no goddess, real or mythological, but the most beautiful of all of God's creatures, clad in hues of beautiful blues: Blessed Mary, the Mother of God. And Mary was not alone but was accompanied by her husband Joseph and by the apostles and a host of heavenly saints. She is there to help us recall the next part of the Eucharistic Prayer, that of the Intercessions. Here, the priest asks Mary and all the saints to intercede on our behalf for the good of the Church and those living on earth, and for the good of the dead.

Finally, you'll recall that next to one of the saints, St. Dominic, in fact, was a big dog, a dachshund to be precise. The dachshund is simply there to remind us of the last part of the Eucharistic Prayer called the Concluding Doxology. Here the priest proclaims:

Through him, and with him, and in him,[10]
O God, almighty Father,
in the unity of the Holy Spirit,
all glory and honor is yours,
forever and ever.

We answer: Amen.

This amen has long been called the Great Amen; so great is the mystery that it affirms. So now, as the great mystery of faith has taken place and Jesus is before us, we might recall the words that he told us himself:

---

10 I can hardly hear these words anymore without thinking as well of my friend Shane Kapler's fascinating study of just what it means to *pray* through, with, and in Jesus. Kapler's study is most aptly titled *Through, With, and In Him: The Prayer Life of Jesus and How to Make It Our Own* (Kettering, OH: Angelico Press, 2014).

> Amen, amen, I say to you, unless you eat the flesh of the Son of Man and drink his blood, you do not have life within you. Whoever eats my flesh and drinks my blood has eternal life, and I will raise him on the last day. For my flesh is true food, and my blood is true drink. Whoever eats my flesh and drinks my blood remains in me and I in him (John 6:53-56).

And now in the Mass, as we reach the Communion Rite, we prepare to do exactly as he advised us, to eat his flesh and drink his blood that we might remain in him and he in us so we may attain eternal life.

Communion Rite

When he was not far from the house, the centurion sent friends to him, saying to him, "Lord, do not trouble yourself, for I am not worthy to have you come under my roof...But say the word and let my servant be healed...." When Jesus heard this he marveled at him, and turned and said to the multitude that followed him, "I tell you, not even in Israel have I found such faith." And when those who had been sent returned to the house, they found the slave well.

Luke 7:6-10

Our Father's Family Room

Our last chapter's location 23, the head of the dining room table, was the most challenging location of all, requiring a full six images. This is not all out of line, since in the sixth chapter of John, Christ proclaimed a truly "hard saying" that would later be desc ribed by a rather hard concept to wrap our limited minds around, that of *transubstantiation*.[1] Our most challenging memory work is behind us as we move right on through our

1 Again, for a more detailed consideration, see Appendix C: Christ's Real Presence in the Eucharist.

memory house, still within the dining room and now at the next and last chair. At the seat on the right (location 24), who should be there but *your own father* with his hands locked in prayer.

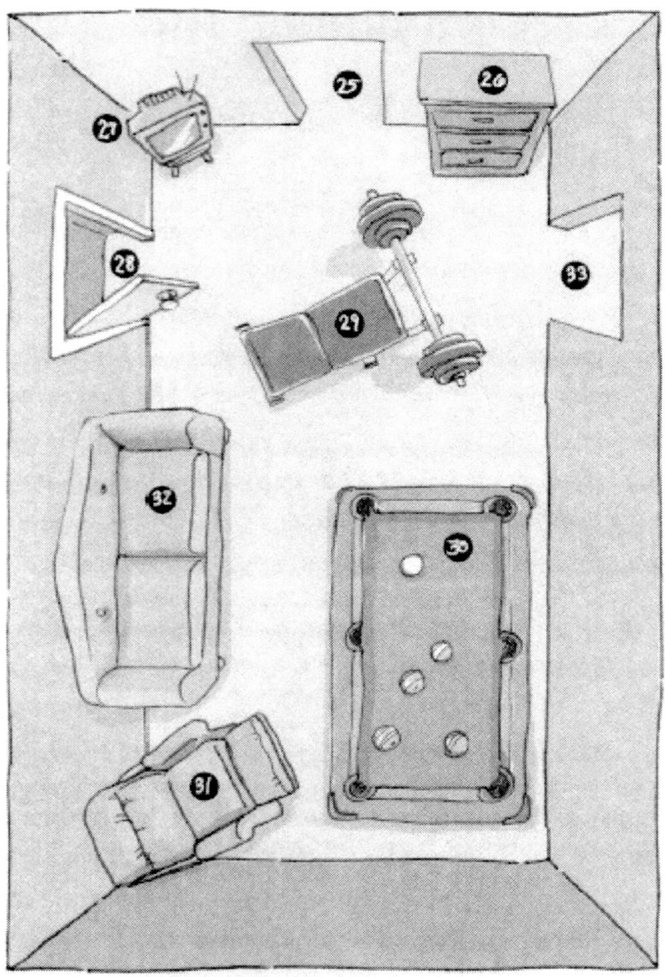

The Family Room

Moving now from the dining room to the adjoining family room, you find at the doorway to the family room (location 25), suspended from the doorframe a gigantic dangling *peace sign.* As you walk into the family room you notice a tall dresser (location 26) in the corner right next to the door. There's a most unusual animal resting on top of it, a pure white *lamb,* crowned with a golden halo. On the other side of the door, in our 27th location, is a small television and as you look at the screen, it displays *an engraved invitation* with your name on the front. As it opens up it reveals a huge *broken host.* Next to the television is a closet (location 28), and when you open it up you find to your surprise that it reveals a whole line of people kneeling at an old-fashioned *altar rail.* Next to the closet sits an exercise bench (location 29), and here you see *yourself* facing toward the back of it as you too *kneel in prayer.* (How funny that it had never occurred to you how much a bench at high incline resembles an old-fashioned kneeler. Come to think of it, it hadn't occurred to me until now either!)

LOCATION	*IMAGE(S)*	PART OF MASS
24. Seat on right	*Your father praying*	The Lord's Prayer (Our Father)
25. Doorway to family room	*Peace sign*	Sign of Peace
26. Dresser	*Lamb with halo*	Lamb of God
27. Television	*Invitation with broken host*	Invitation to Communion
28. Closet	*Altar rail*	Communion
29. Exercise bench	*You kneeling/ praying*	Prayer after Communion

24. The Lord's Prayer

At the seat on the right (24), the last location in the dining room, we saw your own father deep in prayer. I saw mine too, and the reason we saw our fathers, was to remind us of the Our Father.

Christ told us that if we are to bring a gift to the altar, we must first be sure we've been reconciled if we have had conflict with anyone (Matt 5:23-24). Now, before we receive the greatest gift of all, we stand in the nave, and upon the altar the priest declares:

> "At the Savior's command and formed by divine teaching we dare to say…"

Next, we join with the priest and all pray out loud in the very word's Christ gave us after his disciples had asked him how to pray (Matt 6:9-13; Luke 11:2-4), known in English as the Lord's Prayer or the Our Father.

This prayer has long been considered the perfect prayer in Catholic Tradition, since it is the prayer that Christ gave to us. The fourth and final part of the *Catechism of the Council of Trent* examines the Lord's Prayer and its implications for all Christian prayer, in over one hundred pages. Our current *Catechism of the Catholic Church* does as well, addressing it in over one hundred pages in its part four on Christian Prayer. It starts by describing the Lord's Prayer as "the summary of the whole gospel" (2761). St. Thomas Aquinas was among many great theologians who wrote and preached about this prayer extensively, in one place during a series of Lenten sermons in Naples,[2] and one thing they all have in common is that they address the prayer's "seven petitions" of God:

1. God's name be "hallowed,"
2. "thy kingdom come,"
3. "thy will be done,"
4. "give us this day our daily bread,"

---

2 See *The Aquinas Catechism: A Simple Explanation of the Catholic Faith by the Church's Greatest Theologian* (Manchester, NH: Sophia Institute Press, 2000).

5. "forgive us our trespasses as we forgive our trespassers,"
6. "lead us not into temptation," and
7. "deliver us from evil."

Each petition is full of theological and spiritual richness and is worth reading about and meditating upon in-depth. Indeed, it did not occur to me fully when writing about the seven deadly sins[3] that within the various parts and petitions of the Lord's Prayer are calls for remedies for each of those deadly sins, as I'll now explain:

"Our Father" *(we pray to "our," not "my," Father for a remedy for envy, which is the experience of being self-absorbed and saddened by another's good, since it reminds us we are all members of the same family, brothers and sisters of the same loving Father, and we pray for the benefit of all),* "who art in heaven" *(a remedy for sloth, which is mired in earthly concerns, neglecting heavenly things and the holiness of God)*, "hallowed be thy name" *(a remedy for vainglory in which we seek earthly glory for our own names and neglect the honor due God),* "thy kingdom come, thy will be done on earth as it is in heaven" *(a remedy for pride, that font from which all the deadly sins flow, in which our will and desires come first),* "give us this day our daily bread" *(both a remedy for gluttony, which seeks more than a day's worth of bread at a time, and for avarice, which seeks more than one's share of any earthly goods – as well as a reminder of the greatest of all breads which we receive in the Eucharist),* "and forgive us our trespasses, as we forgive those who trespass against us" *(a remedy against the unforgiving anger of wrath).* "Lead us not into temptation, but deliver us from evil" *(a remedy against the temptations of lust and every kind of evil that comes from deadly sins).*

3 Kevin Vost, *The Seven Deadly Sins: A Thomistic Approach to Vanquishing Vice and Sin* (Manchester, NH: Sophia Institute Press, 2015).

After the conclusion of the Lord's Prayer, the priest declares:

Deliver us, Lord, we pray, from every evil, graciously grant us peace in our days, that, by the help of your mercy, we may be always free from sin and safe from distress, as we await the blessed hope of the coming of our Savior, Jesus Christ.

We respond:

For the kingdom, and the power and the glory are yours now and for ever.

25. Sign of Peace

Now we enter our father's family room, and dangling from the door (25) we saw a huge peace sign, reminding us, of course, of the sign of peace. Five times in Sts. Paul's and Peter's letters they advise Christians to greet one another with a "holy kiss" or a "kiss of love."[4] The early Church Fathers long recognized this "sign of peace," and the words used in the exchange echo an old Jewish greeting employed by Christ himself: "Peace be with you!"[5] Here the Church expresses its peace and unity in this simple rite before we receive Communion:

Priest: Lord Jesus Christ, you said to your Apostles: Peace I leave you, my peace I give you, look not on our sins, but on the faith of your Church, and graciously grant her peace and unity in accordance with your will. Who live and reign for ever and ever.

---

4 Rom 16:16; 1 Cor 16:20; 2 Cor 13:12; 1 Thess 5:26; and 1 Pet 5:14.

5 Luke 24:36; John 20:21; 20:26.

People: Amen.

Priest: The peace of the Lord be with you always.

People: And with your spirit.

Deacon (or Priest): Let us offer each other the sign of peace.

Here, we extend our hand in a handshake of peace, typically to those at our sides and those within arm's reach in the pews in front and behind us, saying Christ's words, "Peace be with you!"

26. Lamb of God

Surely now you will recall that as we entered the family room we first encountered a tall dresser (26) in the corner upon which sat a lamb with a golden halo. That lamb, of course, represents the Lamb of God, Jesus Christ, who takes away the sins of the world. Breaking the host over the paten and placing a small piece in the chalice, the priest prays quietly,

"May this mingling of the Body and Blood of our Lord Jesus Christ bring eternal life to us who receive it." We respond as follows:

> Lamb of God, you take away the sins of the world, have mercy on us.
>
> Lamb of God, you take away the sins of the world, have mercy on us.
>
> Lamb of God, you take away the sins of the world, grant us peace.

Next we kneel and pray in silence while the priest quietly prays one of two prayers:

> Lord Jesus Christ, Son of the living God, who, by the will of the Father and the work of the Holy Spirit, through your Death gave life to the world, free me by this, your most holy Body and Blood, from all my sins and from every evil; keep me always faithful to your commandments, and never let me be parted from you,
>
> OR,
>
> May the receiving of your Body and Blood, Lord Jesus Christ, not bring me to Judgment and condemnation, but through your loving mercy be for me a protection in mind and body and a healing remedy.

27. Invitation to Communion

Upon the screen of the small television set (27) we saw that engraved invitation with the image of a broken host on its cover. That invitation will remind us of the Invitation to Communion wherein we are called to join in the supper of the lamb. The priest now holds the host above the paten, and facing the people, he declares out loud:

> Behold the Lamb of God, behold him who takes away the sins of the world. Blessed are those called to the supper of the Lamb.

The priest and people both then proclaim (echoing the centurion's words in St. Luke, with which we started this chapter):

> Lord, I am not worthy that you should enter under my roof, but only say the word and my soul shall be healed.

The priest then prays silently to himself before consuming the Body of Christ:

> May the Body of Christ keep me safe for eternal life.

Then, before partaking of the Blood of Christ, the priest takes the chalice and prays:

> May the Blood of Christ keep me safe for eternal life.

28. Communion

Now we move on to our closet (28) where inside we saw an old altar rail. The altar rail itself will appear in this book's Part II on the Traditional

Latin Mass. This image, for now, will remind us it's time to line up for Communion, to receive the body and blood, the soul and divinity of Christ from the priest, deacon, or Eucharistic minister either on the tongue or in the hand. In the New Mass, either manner of reception is acceptable. Some people believe reception on the tongue bespeaks a deeper reverence since we do not touch the Real Presence of Christ with our own hands. Those who prefer to take the host reverently in their own hands might meditate upon early fourth-century instructions from the likes of the Eastern Sts. Cyril of Jerusalem and John Chrysostom, both Doctors of the Church, who described making one hand a throne for the other which receives the King.

When the priest, deacon, or extraordinary minister gives us Communion with the host, he or she says: "The Body of Christ." We respond. "Amen." If we choose to receive the Blood of Christ as well, the priest, deacon, or minister says: "The Blood of Christ." We respond. "Amen."

We then cross ourselves, and hands folded in prayer in front of us, return to our seat in the pew, praying and singing the Communion song. When all of the vessels of the Mass have been purified and cleaned upon the altar, the priest or deacon quietly recites this prayer:

> What has passed our lips, as food, O Lord, may we possess in purity of heart, that what has been given us in time may be our healing for eternity.

29. Prayer After Communion

Next we moved to our inclined weightlifting bench (29) and noticed how it looked like a kneeler. This is because after Communion we kneel in prayer until we stand when the priest declares: "Let us pray." The priest then recites a proper prayer for after Communion. Staying with our twenty-fourth Sunday in Ordinary Time example, this is the prayer he prays:

> May the working of this heavenly gift, O Lord, we pray, take possession of our minds and bodies, so that its effects, and not our own desires, may always prevail in us. Through Christ our Lord.
>
> Again, we respond: Amen.

How often do you give the attention and take the time to fully absorb and heed the words of this prayer? Listen closely to the Prayer after Communion, all versions of which pray that in some way we will be benefited and transformed by God's great gift of himself, so that we may go forth to pass on those blessings in our daily lives.

Concluding Rites

Peace be with you. As the Father has sent me, so I send you.
John 20:21

From the Family Room and into the World

The Mass has ended, and perhaps these words trigger in your memory the memorable words "go in peace to love and serve the Lord" that were used prior to the updated translation of the Mass in English that began on November 27, 2011. Well, we have now reached the brief but very important rites that conclude the holy sacrifice of the Mass in the *Novus Ordo*. So memorable are they that the very name of Mass derives from the words of the rite in Latin, *"Ite missa, est,"* meaning "the Mass is ended" or more literally, "Go, this is the dismissal." In a sense though, the Mass never ends here on earth, since it is constantly prayed somewhere in the world and since we are always called to carry it out into the world at the conclusion of every Mass we attend.

Back to our mnemonic tour of our family room: after the incline weight bench, we arrive at the eight-foot pool table (30), and here we see King *Solomon,* in all of his glory, giving us a *solemn blessing.* Let's imagine him with a flowing beard, dressed in flowing vestments, with a crown on his head, and calling out from the steps of his great temple – all from atop our lowly pool table! Next to the pool table is a comfortable recliner (31), and sitting on top of it you feel most *blessed* to see your last *final* exam from some class you've just taken, just laid there by the teacher, and complete with a big red A+! Last and certainly not least, we move to the family room couch (32), and here we find a stern *army sergeant* who rises and yells right at us, *"Dismissed!"* Now let's review.

LOCATION	***IMAGE(S)***	**PART OF MASS**
30. Pool Table	*Solomon makes sign of cross*	Solemn blessing
31. Recliner	*Teacher blesses your final exam*	Final blessing
32. Couch	*Army Sgt. bellows "Dismissed!"*	Dismissal

So ends the tour of the family room and the whole house, but before we close Part I of this book, let's find out what these final images mean in terms of the Holy Mass.

30. Solemn Blessing

The reason for King Solomon upon our pool table (30) is that after a period of time seated in silent prayer after Communion, the priest rises and gives us not a Solomon but a solemn blessing.

Priest: The Lord be with you.

We respond: And with your spirit.

31. Final Blessing

Resting on the recliner (31), that final exam on which we did so well reminds us of the final blessing.

Priest (while he and we make the sign of the cross): May almighty God bless you, the Father, and the Son, and the Holy Spirit.

We respond: Amen.

32. Dismissal

Finally, we arrived at the family room sofa (32). Usually a quite comforting site, this time we saw a bellicose army sergeant arise and bellow at us, "Dismissed!" His dismissal, of course, is merely to remind us of the priest or deacon's dismissal, the last rite of the New Mass. We all remain standing while the priest or deacon gives one of four versions of the dismissal, either "Go forth, the Mass is ended," "Go and announce the Gospel of the Lord," "Go in peace, glorifying the Lord by your life," or simply,

"Go in peace." Regardless of which version is pronounced, we respond, "Thanks be to God."

At this point too, we should meditate upon our own words, thinking about and feeling that gratitude with such an intensity that we burn to go out and do what we have just been bidden – to go out into the world proclaiming Christ's good news by promoting peace and glorifying God by the way that we live our lives, a way that proclaims to others that Christ now lives within us.

Well, the memory tour of the *Novus Ordo* Mass has ended. Now it is time to go forth and live that Mass's lessons while we prepare for our next Mass, be it next week, or ideally tomorrow. Have you memorized all the essential parts now, literally forward and backward? The best way to rehearse and to practice them is to hear and to live them every time you go to Mass. With repeated exposure and focused attention, you'll hardly need our memory images to remember the names and the order of those parts. With more time still, even the words and the meanings of the prayers will find their way deep into your mind and heart.

Our memory work is far from over though, even within the pages of this book. Now that we are armed (or really, *minded* I suppose) with the parts of the *Novus Ordo*, it is time to go back to our roots to participate in, enjoy and relish, and yes, to memorize too the parts of the Extraordinary Form, the Traditional Latin Mass.

–Part II–

Remembering and Treasuring the Traditional Latin Mass

Treasures, however great and precious, are never appreciated until examined, counted over, and summed up. Hence it is, dear reader, that by many there is formed no due estimate of the holy and awful sacrifice of the Mass. Though the greatest treasure which glories and enriches the Church of God, it is still a hidden treasure, and known to few. Ah, if this jewel of paradise were but known, who would not give up all things to obtain it!

St. Leonard of Port Maurice[1]

1 St. Leonard of Port Maurice, *The Hidden Treasure: Holy Mass* (Rockford, IL: TAN Books, 1980), 17.

Prologue to Part II

"There is no contradiction between the two editions of the Roman Missal. In the history of the liturgy there is growth and progress, but no rupture. What earlier generations held as sacred, remains sacred and great for us too, and it cannot all of a sudden be entirely forbidden or even considered harmful. It behooves all of us to preserve the riches which have developed in the Church's faith and prayer, and to give them their proper place.

"It has clearly been demonstrated that young persons too have discovered this liturgical form, felt its attraction and found in it a form of encounter with the Mystery of the Most Holy Eucharist particularly suited to them."

Pope Benedict XVI[2]

When it comes to the Holy Mass, our time, in many ways, is a great time to be a Catholic. In Part I we examined the *Novus Ordo Missae,* the New Mass in the vernacular promulgated by Pope Paul VI in 1969. The Mass is easy to follow in one's own language and allows for considerable exterior participation in the form of many verbal responses and the interpersonal gesture of the sign of peace.

2 Pope Benedict XVI, Letter to the Bishops on the Occasion of the Publication of the Apostolic Letter 'Motu Proprio Data' *Summorum pontificum* On the Use of the Roman Liturgy Prior to the Reform of 1970 (7 July 2007).

Still, as Pope Benedict XVI made crystal clear on July 7, 2007, in his Letter to the Bishops and the accompanying Apostolic Letter *Summorum pontificum,* the Traditional Latin Mass that developed throughout the Church's history, was standardized by St. Pope Pius V in 1570, and was last modified and promulgated by St. Pope John XXIII in the 1962 Roman missal remains a valid and most cherished part of our living Catholic Tradition. He declared that they are not two different rites of the Mass, but the Ordinary Form (*Novus Ordo*) and the Extraordinary Form (Traditional Latin Mass) of the Roman rite of the Mass.

Growing numbers of us in our day are blessed with the opportunity to glorify God through our participation in *both* of these rites, if we should choose to do so. In my own small city of Springfield in Central Illinois, in addition to several churches offering the Ordinary Form of the Mass daily, one parish church offers the Latin Extraordinary Form on Saturday mornings, and another parish was blessed by our bishops' invitation to three priests—Canons of St. John Cantius—to come to town from Chicago and administer a combined parish with two churches. They now offer both forms of Mass daily (and some Spanish-language Masses too)! Another church in our diocese offers a Latin Mass on Saturdays only. If you are not aware of one in your area, you might consider checking the Internet for the nearest Latin Mass to you as it would well be worth at least an occasional drive even if some distance away.

The Traditional Latin Mass is a most beautiful thing, remembered and cherished by many priests, religious, and lay persons who grew up with it, as well as by young people who have discovered its hidden treasures. It can also be a bit daunting though for those of us who grew up under the Ordinary Form. I attended the Latin Mass during my own childhood years but have only the vaguest memories, since the New Order Mass replaced it when I was nine years old. In rediscovering the Latin Mass, I have seen that it can prove difficult to follow, even when guided by a missal, partly because so much of the Mass, especially the Low Mass I've usually attended, is carried out in a beautiful, reverent silence.

Hopefully the pages of Part II will help open up the Extraordinary Form, complete with its extraordinary opportunities for interior participation in the glorious sacrifice of the Mass. Though it is not necessary, I would encourage readers who are new to the Latin Mass to obtain and follow along as well with a Latin-English Booklet Missal.[3] Further, I will note again that in laying out forty-two parts, I followed the headings in Dom Prosper Gueranger, O.S.B.'s *Explanation of the Holy Mass.* That book may also be a valuable resource in helping you to come to know and love the Latin Mass. Note well that there are distinctions between the more complete and elaborate High Mass and the more common and routine Low Mass. Most of the rites we will focus on appear in the Low Mass, though at times I will note the exceptions.

With that said, let us then "go up to the altar" to share in the great mystery of the greatest sacrifice of all.

3 A simple one I use and that is commonly used in my city and which I have relied on both at Latin Mass and within the pages of this book is the *Latin-English Booklet Missal For Praying the Traditional Latin Mass: Commemorative Edition in Thanksgiving for 'Summorum pontificum'* (Chicago: Coalition in Support of Ecclesia Dei, 2015).

Mass of the Catechumens

"Holy Mass is the sun of all spiritual exercises, the mainspring of devotion, the soul of piety, the fire of divine charity, the abyss of divine mercy and a precious means whereby God confers upon us His graces."
St. Francis de Sales, *Introduction to a Devout Life*[1]

Once again I cordially invite you into the rooms of our memory house. This time as you approach the door some things seem quite familiar, and yet other things seem rather strange. It's the right house, all right. The street address is still four, yet the first time it was written as "4," and now it is written as "IV." The house also appears much older than you had remembered. You are a bit perplexed perhaps, but certainly undaunted. You knock on the front door (location 1) since there is no electric doorbell, and to your surprise you are greeted by old *King David* himself. You can tell by the crown on his head and the slingshot attached to his belt. He blesses you with the s*ign of the cross,* and then, oddly enough, he asks you to judge him, bellowing out: *"Adjudicate me!"*

Moving inside to our familiar doormat (2) you spy an even stranger scene. A *convict* (you can tell by his black and white striped jumpsuit – or orange, if you prefer) is *fitting* a similar garment on Winnie the Pooh's donkey friend *Eeyore.* (Odd indeed, but you'll soon see the reason behind

1 Cited in Martin von Cochem, *The Incredible Catholic Mass* (Charlotte, NC: TAN Books, 2012), 16.

the madness.) Looking back out through the glass panel next to the door (3), you notice that the front yard has been completely enveloped in a dense cloud of *incense.* You see it coming in through the crack beneath the front door, and you find its aroma is absolutely heavenly. In the picture on the wall next to the door (also known as location 4), you see depicted an old car with a big sign underneath it that says *"Made in Detroit,"* except that the "Made" and the "D" in Detroit have all but faded away over time.

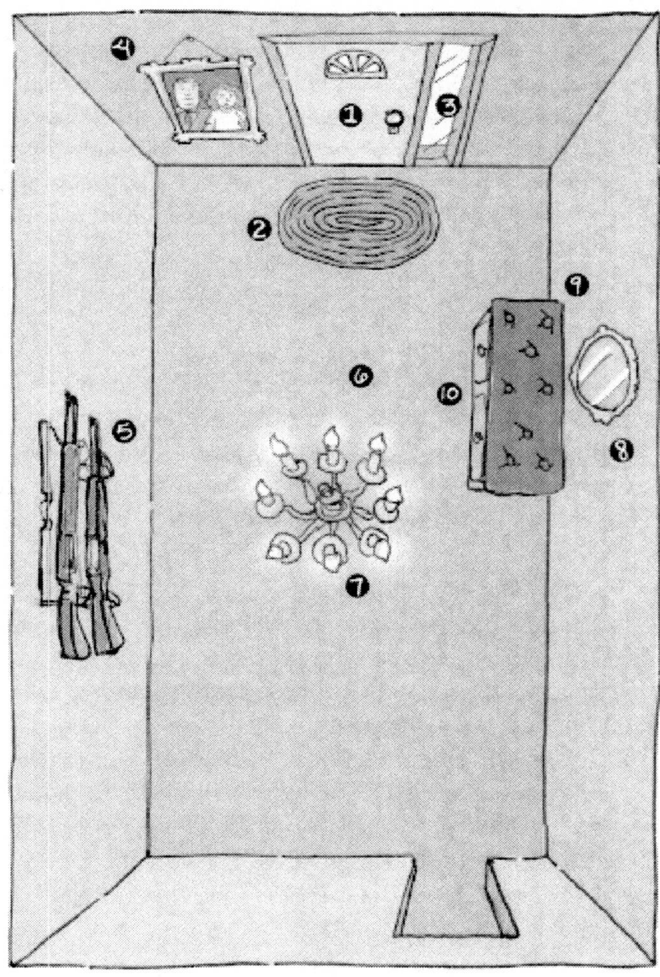

The Foyer

On next to the gun rack (5) and we come across a familiar and comforting sight, those very same *Valkyries* we saw there during our first tour through this house. That brings us to location 6 in the center of the foyer, and here again we are greeted by a most familiar sight, for here again is that singer, friend, or even old flag, named *Gloria.* Up now travel our eyes to the chandelier (7), and for the third location in a row, we stand on familiar ground, for there is that *collection basket* brimming over with prayers.

We move over to the mirror now (8), and things are a little different. The mirror seems older and cloudier, and there, instead of the first-grade reader we saw in it the last time, is a much more disconcerting sight. A *letter* is inside the mirror, and on it sits a *pistol* emblazoned with a large letter *"E."* Beneath the mirror sits the little cushioned bench (9), and upon that bench sits a young *graduate* you know by the name of *Al,* cap and gown and all. The next thing you know though, he stands up and starts to climb some *stairs* that you had not realized were there. In the drawer in the bench (10) you see an even stranger sight, for there is *Al* again, this time with his friend *Lulu.* (How do we know she's named Lulu? Well, it says it on her shirt!) Within that little drawer, they are having a grand old time circling around a tiny toy train *track.*

Moving from the foyer to the center of the living room (11), you notice a stream of gold objects cascading from the ceiling and forming a glowing and glittering pile on the floor. Upon closer inspection you see that the golden, coin-like discs are decorative *sequins.* Now you spy through the picture window (12) into the backyard. How interesting that the little saplings you noticed the first time through the house are now full-grown towering oaks! What truly captures your attention though is that our familiar *newsboy* has climbed to the very top of one of them, proclaiming to all his *"Good News!"* Finally, you are relieved to see him safely climb down, and your gaze returns to the living room sofa (13). Here sit those familiar *professional fates* arranged, in your opinion, into a very *nice scene.*

And so ends the mnemonic tour of this chapter. Please rehearse a bit and see if you can reel them off: (1) King David saying "Adjudicate me!", (2) the con fitting Eyeore, (3) incense, (4) car made in Detroit, (5) Valkyries, (6) Gloria, (7) collection basket, (8) letter with pistol with "E," (9) graduate Al, (10) Al and Lulu on the track, (11) sequins, (12) "Good News!" boy, and (13) professional fates in nice scene. Better yet, can you say them backward? Now, let's take a peek at what we've memorized before we spell out all that it means.

LOCATION	*IMAGE*	PART OF MASS
1. Front door	*King David signs cross, says, "Adju-dicate me!"*	Judica Me
2. Doormat	*Con fits Eeyore*	Confiteor
3. Glass panel next to door	*Cloud of incense*	Incensing the altar
4. Picture on wall	*Car made in De-troit, faded D*	Introit
5. Gun rack	*Valkyries*	*Kyrie*
6. Center of foyer	*Singer or friend named Gloria (or "Old Glory")*	*Gloria*
7. Chandelier	*Collection basket full of prayers*	Collect
8. Mirror	*Pistol with E rests on letter*	Epistle
9. Bench	*Graduate named Al goes up stairs*	Gradual
10. Drawer	*Al and Lulu on train track*	Alleluia or Tract
11. Center of living room	*Giant golden se-quins trickle down*	Sequence
12. Picture window	*Newsboy pro-claims "Good news!"*	Gospel
13. Sofa	*Fates in nice scene*	Credo (Profession of Faith/Nicene Creed)

1. Judica Me

As we approached the front door (1) for the second time, surely you'll recall that King David himself greeted us and asked us to judge him, calling out to us, "Adjudicate me!" This image cannot fail to bring to mind the first part of the Latin Mass known as the *Judica Me.*[2] This first rite takes place right after the priest declares the sign of the cross in Latin: *"In nomine Patris, +*[3] *et Filii, et Spiritus Sancti. Amen."* Then he declares, *"Introibo ad altare Dei,"* to which the server responds, *"Ad Deum qui laetificat juventutem meam."*

The first words of the Judica Me are, as you may have guessed, well, *"Judica me,"* as in "Judge me," and further, "Judge me, O God, and distinguish my cause from the nation that is not holy; deliver me from the unjust and deceitful man." These words are based on Psalm 42,[4] largely because of the words that the priest has already prayed and which the server will now pray once again – *"Introibo ad altare Dei,"* "I will go in unto the Altar of God." The priest's words, *"Emitte lucem tuam, et veritatem tuam,"* "Send forth Thy light and Thy truth," also echo the Psalm, and the server's response includes the words, *"Ad Deum qui laetificat juventutem meam,"* "unto God, Who giveth joy to my youth," again echoing the words of David. The priest also declares, *"Gloria Patri, et Filio, et Spiritui Sancto,"* to which the server responds, *"Sicut erat in prinicipio et nunc, et semper, et in saecula saeculorum. Amen."* These are the words familiar to us in the "Glory Be": "Glory be to the Father, and to the Son, and to the Holy Spirit. As it was in the beginning, is now, and ever shall be, world without end. Amen."

Dom Gueranger reports that the *Judica Me* was not in ancient missals, but its usage was established by St. Pope Pius V in 1568. We kneel during this holy dialogue between the priest and the server. What a beauti-

---

2 Before High Masses the rite of *Asperges,* or sprinkling of holy water, is first performed. (See part 3 of the Sprinkling of Holy Water in the Ordinary Form for additional details.)

3 This symbol represents the many times throughout the Mass when the priest makes the sign of the cross.

4 Psalm 42 in the Latin Vulgate is Psalm 43 in the versions including the New American Bible (NAB) and the Revised Standard Version (RSV). Verse four refers to going to the altar of God, which gave the young psalmist David exceeding joy.

ful way to open the Mass, as the priest prepares to ascend the altar, re-presenting the sacrifice Christ offered us on the altar of Mount Calvary to bring to us the prospect of exceeding joy and everlasting life. Have we prepared our hearts and minds to ascend that altar with him?

2. Confiteor

At our entrance mat, we saw that odd scene of a prison convict fitting a garment for the fictional donkey Eeyore. Silly as it may seem, the con fitting Eeyore is a pretty straightforward reminder of the sounds of the Latin word *Confiteor.* But what does it mean in the context of the holy sacrifice of the Mass? *"Confiteor Deo Omnipotenti,"* "I confess to Almighty God," are the words that open this prayer that may date back to the eighth century. It corresponds to the longer penitential rite (location 4) of the Ordinary Form of the Mass. (If you would care to lock in the meaning of confession with the image for the *Confiteor,* I suggest you simply also imagine the "con" fitting Eeyore confessing his crime as he fits him.)

There are differences between the prayers of penitence in the New and Old Masses, however. The *Confiteor* confesses sins not only to God and to our brothers and sisters, but to the Blessed Virgin Mary, Michael the Archangel, Blessed John the Baptist, Sts. Peter and Paul, and all the saints, seeking their saintly intercession.

The *Confiteor* also includes the words *"mea culpa,"* "through my fault," three times, while the priest strikes his breast three times, like the tax collector who "beat his breast and prayed, 'O God, be merciful, to me, a sinner'" (Luke 18:13). The priest then gives the absolution in words that begin, *"Misereatur vestri omnipotens Deus, et dismissis peccatis vestris, perducat vos ad vitam aeternam,"* "May Almighty God have mercy upon you, forgive you your sins, and bring you to life everlasting." The server responds, *"Amen."*

3. Incensing the Altar

As we looked out the glass panel (3) into the front yard, we saw the air was filled with a cloud of incense. Indeed, it spilled in to us under the front door with the most heavenly aroma. This image represents the incensing of the altar that the priest performs at this point during a High Mass. The priest uses a *thurible,* a brass instrument, often gold-plated, hanging from a chain to disperse burning incense about the altar. The practice goes back to the rituals of the temple. "The priest shall also put some of the blood on the horns of the altar of fragrant incense which stands before the LORD in the tent of meeting" (Lev 4:7). The altar represents Christ and contains the relics of saints. The incense shows reverence, symbolizes the sanctifying grace of the Holy Spirit, and the prayers of the saints, as well. "Let my prayer be incense before you; my uplifted hands an evening offering" (Ps 141:2). We also incense on the altar on earth in imitation of the angels in heaven: "Another angel came and stood at the altar, holding a gold censer. He was given a great quantity of incense to offer, along with the prayers of all the holy ones, on the gold altar that was before the throne" (Rev 8:3).

4. Introit

In the picture on the foyer back wall (4) we saw an old car with a sign that said "Made in Detroit," though the "Made in" and the "D" in "Detroit" had all but faded away. This was to recall the sounds of the word *"Introit."* The Latin word means "entrance," and the priest, having ascended the altar, reads the proper (changing) prayer of the Introit from the "epistle side" (the left side of the altar from the perspective of the altar cross, the right side from the congregation's perspective). The missal booklet that I use and referenced earlier refers at this point to Tobias 12:6.[5] That verse reads: "Bless God and give him thanks before all the living for the good things he has done for you, by blessing and extolling his name in song. Proclaim before all with due honor the deeds of God, and do not be slack in thanking him." The particular sample *Introit* in my missal begins, *"Benedicta sit sancta Trinitas,"* "Blessed be the holy Trinity," and includes within it the words of the "Glory Be" prayer, as we heard before during the first part of the Mass in the *Judica Me.*

5. Kyrie

And next you heard those stirring strains of Wagner when at the *gun rack* in the foyer (location 5) you saw the flight of the *Valkyries.* Now we examine the phrase or the song you really do hear at Mass, because it is time for the *Kyrie.* (Indeed, we might as well imagine those Valkyries praying the *Kyrie* too!) If those last three sentences seem a little familiar, it is because they are. Indeed, they were copied and pasted from the same fifth location of the Ordinary Form of the Mass. That should make things simple. We pray the *Kyrie* here in the fifth location too, but we could say that we pray it three times as much! Here is how the *Kyrie* is prayed in the Latin Mass:

Priest: *Kyrie, eleison.*
Server: *Kyrie, eleison.*
Priest: *Kyrie, eleison.*
Server: *Christe eleison.*
Priest: *Christe eleison.*
Server: *Christe eleison.*
Priest: *Kyrie eleison.*
Server: *Kyrie eleison.*
Priest: *Kyrie eleison.*

In this prayer, the Church implores for mercy from the Holy Trinity. The first three proclamations of *"Kyrie eleison"* address the Lord as God the Father; the next three proclamations of *"Christe eleison"* address the

5 Tobit in the NAB and many other translations.

Lord as Christ, God the Son; and the final three proclamations of *"Kyrie eleison"* address the Lord as the Holy Spirit. As we hear this ninefold dialogue of prayer between the priest and the server we would do well to recall how it mimics on earth the nine choirs of angels who sing to the Holy Trinity in heaven.

6. Gloria

Next, we moved to the center of the foyer (6) where we saw the famous singer, dear friend, or even the old flag that reminded us of the *Gloria,* and again we are on familiar ground, for the *Gloria* appeared in the same location in the New Order of the Mass. The main differences here are that this prayer is proclaimed in Latin and (outwardly anyway) by the priest alone. *"Gloria in excelsis Deo"* he begins, *"et in terra pax homnibus bonae voluntatis."* "Glory be to God on high and on earth peace to men of good will." The whole English text of the prayer was presented in Part I. Please see a Latin missal, or better yet, attend a Mass in the Extraordinary Form to hear this glorious prayer of praise and thanks to God. (As is the case in the Ordinary Form, the *Gloria* is not proclaimed during Lent, Advent, and Masses for the Dead.)

7. Collect

Again we found up in the foyer's chandelier (7) a collection basket brimming over not with money but with prayers. For the third location in a row, the old Latin Mass parallels the new vernacular Mass, for here we come again to the C*ollect* or the Opening Prayer, that four-parted prayer that calls upon God the Father or the Son, recalls one of God's great deeds, makes a request of God, and declares that our prayer is made through Christ's mediation. This prayer is a proper that changes with each Mass. The missal that I use provides an example that begins with the words *"Omnipotens sempiterne Deus,"* "Almighty and Everlasting God." Let's read it right now in English, watching for those four parts, and praising the almighty God all the while:

Almighty and Everlasting God, by Whose gift Thy servants, in confessing the true Faith, acknowledge the glory of the Eternal Trinity, and adore the Unity in the power of Thy Majesty: grant that by steadfastness in the same Faith we may evermore be defended from all adversities. Through our Lord Jesus Christ Thy Son, Who liveth and reigneth with Thee in the unity of the Holy Ghost, God for ever and ever.

Server: *Amen.*

8. Epistle

In this second tour of our memory house, at the site of the foyer's mirror (8), we saw not the first-grade reader as we did last time to remind us of the first reading, but instead a much more unusual image, that of a letter with a pistol with a large "E" on it, and that "E pistol" is there merely to remind us of the Epistle. In the Traditional Latin Mass, at least for the last one thousand years or so, there has only been one Scripture reading prior to the Gospel, and that from the New Testament, most often from the letters (i.e., epistles) of St. Paul. It is read, as you might suspect, from the epistle side of the altar while the congregation sits (as is the case in the *Novus Ordo*). It is also a proper reading that changes with each Mass according to the day of the liturgical season.

So then, so far, the words of the Prophet David have prepared the ascent to the altar, and an apostle has spoken to us of the Word of God. Very soon within the order of the Mass we'll hear the words of the Word Himself.

9. Gradual

Underneath the mirror upon the cushioned bench (9), you will recall your friend Al wearing a graduation cap and gown and climbing up some steps. Now let's see what he was doing there. The graduate Al was climbing those steps to remind us of the *Gradual.* The *Gradual* is another proper prayer that changes with each Mass, but in each variation it prepares us for the Gospel; it gained its named from the Gradual Psalms which the ancient Jews would sing as they climbed up the steps of the Temple. The example provided in the missal booklet I use starts, *"Benedictus es, Domine, qui intueris abyssos, et sedes super Cherubim,"* "Blessed art Thou, O Lord, that beholdest the depths and sittest above the Cherubim."

What beautiful, heavenly imagery here! It calls to mind quite clearly again that the Mass recapitulates the heavenly Mass of the angels and saints, where God sits above the nine choirs of angels, the Cherubim being those of the second-highest rank.[6]

10. Alleluia (or Tract)

In the small drawer of the cushioned bench we saw Al again, and this time with Lulu. They are there, of course, to remind us of the *Alleluia.* We came across the Alleluia in the New Mass at location 11 for the Gospel acclamation. In Latin, it goes *"Alleluia, alleluia. Benedictus es, Domine, Deus partum nostrorum, et laudabilis in saecula. Alleluia,"* which is rendered in English "Alleluia, alleluia. Blessed art Thou, O Lord, the God of our fathers, and worthy to be praised for ever. Alleluia." Keeping the heavenly nature of the Holy Mass in mind, we might do well to recall the multitudes in heaven, proclaiming again and again around God's throne a full four times, *"Alleluia! Alleluia! Alleluia! Alleluia!"* (Rev 19:1, 3, 4, & 6).

You might recall as well that Al and Lulu were on a train track. The track reminds us of the *Tract,* a prayer that is used in lieu of the *Alleluia* during mournful seasons such as Lent. Its name comes from the Latin word *tractus,* meaning "flowing or continuous," and it is often excerpted from one of the Psalms.

11. Sequence

Recall now the shower of golden sequins raining down in the center of the living room (11). Prayers come next known as the Sequence, since they follow on, but only during certain liturgical feasts of the year: Five

6 The highest tier consists of the Seraphim, Cherubim, and Thrones; the middle tier consists of the Dominions, Thrones, and Virtues; and the last of the Principalities, Archangels, and Angels. For a fascinating look at these choirs of angels, building upon the writings of the Scriptures, Dionysius, and Pope St. Gregory the Great, see St. Thomas Aquinas' *Summa theologica,* I, q. 108.

recited or sung in the Mass are the *Victimae Paschali* at Easter, the *Veni Sancte Spiritus* at Pentecost, the *Lauda Sion* for *Corpus Christi*, the *Stabat Mater*, and the *Dies Irae*.[7]

12. Gospel

And now we come to the words of the Word, the Gospel of our Lord Jesus Christ. This is why we saw our familiar good newsboy through the picture window (12), proclaiming good news out in the backyard. Moving from our memory tour back to the church and the Holy Mass, the priest's missal has now been moved to the right, the Gospel side of the altar (the left from our perspective in the nave). The priest, bowed and with hands joined in prayer, first recites a prayer known as the "*Munda Cor Meum.*" Picture him, if you'd like, rubbing a bar of soap over his heart, because these words mean "cleanse my heart." The pure of heart will see God (Matt 5:8), and the pure of heart will proclaim his Gospel as well. His call for cleansing and purification also includes the cleansing of his lips, recalling the words of Isaiah 6:5-7. Here, in English, are the words of the prayer:

> Cleanse my heart and my lips, O Almighty God, Who didst cleanse the lips of the prophet Isaias[8] with a burning coal; through Thy gracious mercy so purify me that I may worthily proclaim the holy Gospel. Through Christ Our Lord. Amen.
>
> Grant, O Lord, Thy blessing.
>
> May the Lord be in my heart and on my lips that I may worthily and fittingly proclaim His Gospel. Amen.

Next, the priest prepares to read the day's Gospel (typically in English in American Latin Masses), saying "*Dominus vobiscum,*" "The Lord

---

7 For a famous and most moving rendition of the *Dies Irae* (Day of Wrath) of which I'm aware, listen sometime to the rousing *Dies Irae* of Mozart's *Requiem Mass* in D Minor.

8 The *Latin-English Booklet Missal for Praying the Traditional Latin Mass* uses "Isaias" for "Isaiah" in keeping with the spelling of the prophet's name in the Douay-Rheims translation of the Bible from the Latin Vulgate.

be with you," to which the server answers, *"Et cum spiritu tuo,"* "And with your spirit." The priest recites from which book today's Gospel comes, and as in the *Novus Ordo,* crosses his forehead, lips, and heart, and we do likewise with him.

After reading the Gospel, the priest delivers a homily or sermon, meditating upon the day's readings and perhaps the saint whose feast is on that day. Preaching is such an important act to call people to Christ, to catechize the faithful, and to stir listeners to live out the Gospel message. In the early 1200s, there was a crisis of preaching of sorts in the Church that was addressed at the Lateran Council of 1215. Typically only bishops were preaching regular homilies, and homilies were therefore rare. Rising to the occasion were two new holy religious Orders: St. Francis' Friars Minor and St. Dominic's order, the latter being so focused on preaching that it would be declared the Order of Preachers.

Drawing a bit (two bits actually) from medieval Dominican wisdom on preaching, I'll note that Blessed Humbert of Romans, the order's fifth Master General, wrote an extensive treatise *On the Formation of Preachers* that examines the art and grace of preaching from every imaginable angle. Here is one small bit of his sage advice:

> Preachers will keep their sermons of reasonable length as well, so they don't give their hearers indigestion! Some preach with nothing but *rational arguments*, others with nothing but *anecdotes*, and yet others by *citing authorities.* The good preacher does *all three* in the right proportions. Indeed, when all three work together, the "hook of preaching" hangs from a strong triple line, "a line which no fish can easily break."[9]

Blessed Humbert's contemporary (the patron saint of science, the teacher and mentor of St. Thomas Aquinas, the Bishop of Regensburg, and one of the Doctors of the Church),[10] St. Albert the Great, reportedly preached homilies that were brief and consisted of three main parts:

---

9 Kevin Vost, *Hounds of the Lord: Great Dominican Saints Every Catholic Should Know and Love* (Manchester, NH: Sophia Institute Press, 2015), 42, with quotations citing Simon Tugwell's *Early Dominicans* (New York: Paulist Press, 1980).

10 (How's that for an introduction?)

1. a short and straightforward *literal explanation* of a scriptural passage,
2. an *allegorical and mystical interpretation* of the passage, and
3. a *summary* of the message in clear-cut language, often cast in the form of an easily memorized *prayer* that God would grant the congregation the spiritual fruits that should accrue from pondering and applying his sacred lessons.[11]

Even if the homily we hear at Mass should not be expounded from the likes of a Blessed Humbert or a St. Albert the Great, we would do well to recall that the priest before us appears *in persona Christi,* in the person of Christ, with words guided by the Holy Spirit. We need to listen carefully then to discern God's message for each of us at each Mass.

13. Credo

At our last location within this chapter, we saw those familiar professional fates sitting upon the living room sofa (13), presenting what we thought was a very nice scene. Those fates represent (again) the Profession of Faith, the nice scene, the Nicene Creed, which begins with the words "I believe," which in Latin is simply *"Credo."* The priest recites the *Credo* during Sunday Mass and principal feasts. As we bow when we come to the words "and by the Holy Spirit was incarnate of the Virgin Mary, and became man," the priest genuflects when he recites the words, *"Et incarnates est de Spirito Sancto ex Maria Virgine et Homo Factus est."* At the prayer's end the priest declares, *"Dominus vobiscum,"* "The Lord be with you," and the server responds, *"Et cum spiritu tuo," "And with thy spirit,"* and then the priest says, *"Oremus"* (Let us pray).

And now this chapter has ended; so too has the Mass of the Catechumens. In ancient times, those who had not yet joined the Catholic Church would be dismissed at this point in the Mass, right before the Commencement of the Mass of the Faithful. In our next chapter we turn to that most holy and faith-filled part of the Latin Mass.

---

11 For those who might care to learn more about St. Albert's great homiletics and more, see the chapter on St. Albert in my *Hounds of the Lord,* or St. Albert's complete biography in my *St. Albert the Great: Champion of Faith and Reason.*

Mass of the Faithful

"For from the rising of the sun to its setting
my name is great among the nations, and in every place
incense is offered to my name, and a pure offering;
from my name is great among the nations,
says the LORD of hosts."
Mal 1:11

Still within the living room and right in front of the sofa, we find, as one might expect, a coffee table (location 14), but you probably did not expect to see a seventeenth-century British *Tory* sitting on it, waiting for you to *offer* him not tea and crumpets but some *bread and wine.* Next we come to the location of the big-screen television set (15) though in a house with furnishing this old you are right to expect not to see one. Upon closer inspection, where the big-screen TV sat is now a large rack holding scrolls. As you unroll a scroll a vast cloud of sweet *incense* rises up from it. On now to the fireplace (16), and instead of a set of logs you find a large *bowl* of steaming volcanic *lava,* and you are astonished to see that it's labeled *"for washing hands."* (Undoubtedly, not many germs would survive!) At the living room doorway into the dining room (17), as you might have suspected, you see your friend *Sue,* her little dog *Skippy,* and *Santa Claus* himself eating a *Trinidad* candy.[1]

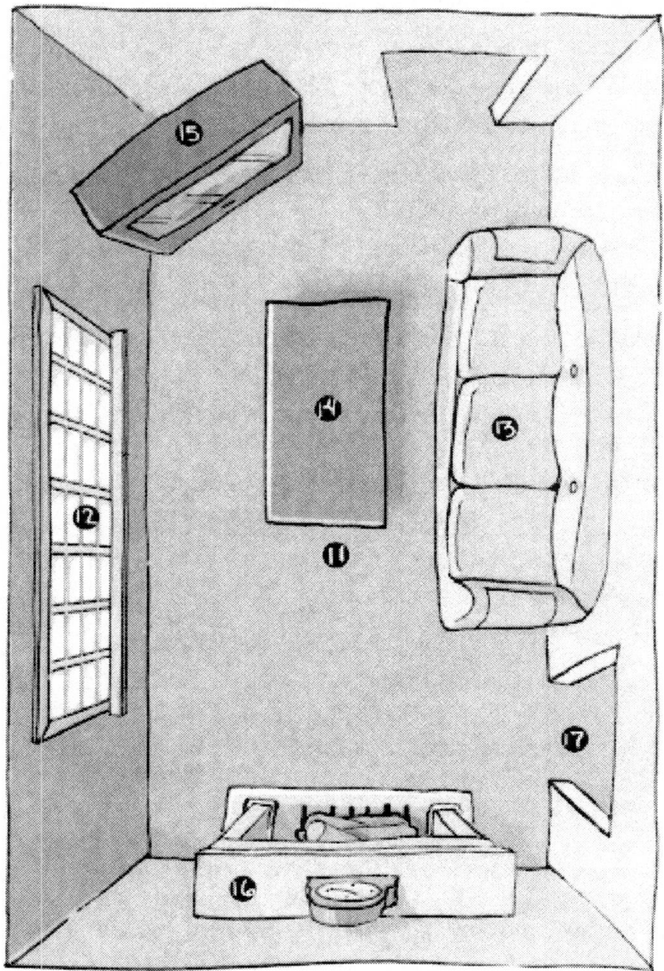

The Living Room

---

1 So maybe you didn't expect that. Not familiar with the Trinidad? Invented by the Fanny May Confections in 1970, it features a dark, creamy chocolate center covered by a golden toasted coconut shell. Try one sometime, but at least an hour before Mass!

And now we enter the dining room of the Mass of the Faithful. At the dining room doorway (18), you find a boat *oar,* a hot cup of *latte,* and a couple *fraternity brothers.* Got all that? At the foot of the dining room table (19) you recognize your own parish *priest's face.* Up on the center of the table (20), as opposed to up on the housetop, again you see a walrus drinking some freeze-dried coffee (*Sanka* to be precise) and he's got some on his *tusk.* And that takes care of this chapter's memory tour. Let's see now how we've done with our memory work, and let's take a peek at just what we have really remembered.

14. Coffee table	*You offer Tory bread and wine*	Offertory
15. Television (scrolls)	*Cloud of incense rises*	Incensing altar, etc.
16. Fireplace	*Lava bowl for washing hands*	Lavabo
17. Living room doorway	*Sue, Skippy, & Santa eat a Trinidad*	Suscipe, Sancta Trinitas
18. Dining room doorway	*Oar, latte, frat brothers*	Orate Fratres
19. Foot of table	*Your priest's face*	Preface
20. Center of table	*Sanka, tusk*	Sanctus

14. Offertory

Still within the living room and right in front of the sofa, we find, as one might expect, a coffee table (location 14), though the rite represented predates coffee drinking by a good thousand years or more! Here we saw a British Tory whom we offered not tea but bread and wine. This unusual scene should serve well to call to mind the rite of the *Offertory,* wherein the priest asks God to receive his offering of bread and wine as Christ

Himself offered them. The Offertory begins the Mass of the Faithful, and the priest begins from the middle of the altar with a proper (changing) Offertory Verse. A sample in the missal booklet I use starts, *"Benedictus sit Deus Pater,"* "Blessed be God, the Father." After this brief *Offertory Verse*, the servers ring a set of bells once, and the priest commences with a series of gestures and prayers that I'll summarize below, for the sake of space, giving only the first few words in Latin, their English translation, and a suggestion for memorization:[2]

Gestures & *First Latin Words*	**English Translation**	**Suggested *Keyword Images* for *Sound* and Meaning**
The priest raises the paten with host saying:		
Suscipe, Sancte Pater...	Accept, O Holy Father...	*Sue, Skippy,* and a *saintly potter* ask their father to accept a gift.
Priest makes sign of cross (+) with paten and places host on corporal. Moves to right side of altar, pouring wine and water into chalice, blessing it before mixed, saying:		

2 I would suggest that you move toward this level of memorization, if you are so inclined, only *after* you have mastered the basic forty-two parts of this Mass. Of course you would do this with the help of a missal, reading the complete prayers and meditating upon their meanings.

Deus + qui humanae sub-stantiae...	O God, + Who in creating man...	*Deuce* card and *key* are handed to a *human* God just gave *sub-stance* to
Returning to the altar's middle, the priest now offers the chalice to God, saying		
Offerimus Tibi...	We offer unto Thee...	You *offer God* an *emus' tibia* bone and a holy chalice
Priest makes + with chal-ice, places it on corporal, covers it with pall and bowing, says:		
In Spiritu Humilitas...	Humbled in Spirit...	You feel *in* you the stir-rings of the Holy *Spirit* while *you* eat some *hum-mus*
The priest raises his eyes and hands and says:		
Veni, Sanctificator omnip-otens...	Come Thou, the Sanctifi-er...	You see a *veiny saint* from *Decatur* who *on* his *knee* holds *patens* and who looks all powerful.

The actions and prayers of this part of the Mass are, as all other parts, ripe with scriptural origins and rich in many levels of meaning. In the prayer beginning *Suscipe Sancte*, for example, consider that the words *"pro omnibus fidelibus christianis vivis atque defunctis,"* "for all faithful Christians, living and dead," proclaim that not only does the Mass honor God, it offers blessings to all Christians living and dead. The mixing of the water and wine, for another example, represents the human and divine natures of Christ. The water suggests the water that flowed from the side of Christ as the wine represents the blood. As for some scriptural roots, note well that in the prayer that commences with *In Spiritu Humilitas,* the words that ask God to find favor with our sacrifice this day reference Daniel 3:39-40: "But with contrite heart and humble spirit let us be received; as though it were burnt offerings of rams and bulls, or tens of thousands of fat lambs, so let our sacrifice be in your presence today and find favor before you; for those who trust in you cannot be put to shame."

We would do well to reflect here too about what goes on with us in the pews while the great offertory goes on at the altar. We noted in part one that caring for the needs of the Church is one of the five basic precepts of the practice of the Catholic faith. When that collection basket is passed, we are provided as well with the opportunity to express and to grow in more than one heavenly virtue.

Gratitude is an obvious one. God has given us everything that we are and all that we have, and He indeed sustains us in existence every moment of our being. Will our monetary offering the next time at Mass express a true heartfelt gratitude?

Another less obvious virtue is that of *magnificence.* The word derives from the Latin *magnus* for "great" and *facere* for "to do or make." Will the contribution we offer up to God at Mass help do and make great things for the glory of God and the aid of our neighbor? It need not be huge, but proportionate to how we abundantly have been gifted with wealth, as we saw in the case of the heavenly weight of the poor widow's penny (Mark 12:41-44; Luke 21:1-4).

15. Incensing altar, etc.

Back now to our memory house's living room and you'll recall that at the site of the big-screen TV (15) we saw an old rack of scrolls in its place. As you unrolled a scroll, a great cloud of incense arose. This image reminds us of the priest blessing the incense and then incensing the offerings of bread and wine, the crucifix, and the altar, while reciting prayers, including Psalm 140 [141], which talks about prayers being like incense before God.

The incensing takes place only at High Mass. Dom Gueringer's book on the *Explanation of the Holy Mass* highlights the fact that many things accompany this rite; Gueringer highlights this fact with a section heading entitled "Incensing the Altar, etc." I can hardly hear the word "etc." without thinking of the musical *The King and I.* The Siamese King learns and develops a love for the Latin word *"etcetera,"* and he ends almost all of his declamations, *"Etcetera, etcetera, etcetera!"* (If the King of Siam can help us remember one way we honor the King of Kings, well, I'm all for calling him to mind.)

16. Lavabo

On now to the fireplace (16) with that fiery bowl of molten lava marked "for washing your hands." Now this image may not sound so extreme for those familiar with that heavy duty hand-cleanser Lava Soap, made with actual pumice (lava rock). What is important, of course, is not our image, but what it represents. *"Lavabo"* means "I will wash." It is the first word of the prayer the priest recites as he washes his hands to symbolize the purity and cleanliness needed to take part in such a holy sacrifice.

"Lavabo inter innocentes manus meas: et circumdabo altare tuum, Domine..." "I will wash my hands among the innocent, and I will encompass Thine Altar, O Lord..." The words of this prayer echo Psalm 25 [26]:6-12 and end with the Glory Be.

We would do well to meditate upon the symbolism of cleansing and purity of the hands. Let's consider for a minute this story from the ancient Irish lore surrounding St. Brigid of Kildare (AD 453-525):

> Out in the fields of Curragh, on one fine summer day, a young student named Ninnidh went running past Brigid at breakneck speed. When asked where he was going, he told her, "I'm going to heaven!" Brigid recited the "Our Father" with him and prophesied that he would become a priest one day and would administer to her the holy viaticum of the Eucharist upon her own deathbed. The formerly frivolous youth devoted himself to his studies and grew steadily toward saintliness. From that day on he would wear a glove on the hand that would deliver to Ireland's patroness her last Communion. This is why he was called Lamh-Gland, "Ninnidh of the clean hand."[3]

3 Kevin Vost, *Three Irish Saints: A Guide to Finding Your Spiritual Style* (Charlotte, NC: TAN Books, 2011), 151.

We might ask ourselves, Are we doing all that we can to keep our hands and our hearts clean for when we receive Jesus for the next time, let alone for our last time on earth?

17. Suscipe, Sancta, Trinitas

Moving along to the living room doorway (17) you saw that odd scene of Sue, Skippy, and Santa Claus eating a Trinidad chocolate. They are there to remind us of the Latin words *"Suscipe, Sancta, Trinitas."* We might imagine them also handing something, perhaps one of those Trinidads, to the Holy Trinity, because those words mean, "Receive, Holy Trinity." These are the first words of the next prayer in the Mass, the Prayer to the Most Holy Trinity. It spells out the reasons for the holy offering in beautiful words well worth presenting here in full translation:

> Receive, O Holy Trinity, this oblation which we make to Thee in memory of the Passion, Resurrection and Ascension of our Lord Jesus Christ; and in honor of blessed Mary ever Virgin, of blessed John the Baptist, the holy Apostles Peter and Paul, of these and of all the Saints. To them let it bring honor, and to us salvation, and may they whom we are commemorating here on earth deign to plead for us in heaven. Through the same Christ our Lord. Amen.

18. Orate Fratres

Over the threshold and into the dining room doorway (18), and now we'll recall the oar and the frat brothers sipping on latte, because this will call to mind the *Orate Fratres.* Picture them praying too, because these words mean "Pray, brethren." This prayer that our sacrifice "may be acceptable to God the Father Almighty" will sound familiar because it also appears in the New Order Mass (recall location 18 there in our first tour of this house and the engraved Invitation to Prayer). So once again, our two memory houses are aligned in locations, calling to mind that while there are significant differences in the parts of the old and new Masses, as Pope Benedict XVI has reminded us, they are two forms of the same Latin Rite. In the Latin Rite the server voices (in Latin) the words that we do in the new, vernacular rite:

> May the Lord accept the Sacrifice from thy hands, to the praise and glory of His Name, for our benefit and for that of all His holy Church.
> Priest (in a low voice): *Amen.*

The priest then quietly recites the Secrets (a proper, changing prayer that asks that God make our offering perfect), and it ends with the same dialogue between the priest and server that took place between the priest and congregation at location 19 in the New Mass, that of the Preface Dialogue.

> Priest (aloud): *Per omnia saecula saeculorum.* (World without end.)

> The people now stand.

> Server: *Amen.*
> Priest: *Dominus vobiscum.* (The Lord be with you.)
> Server: *Et cum spiritu tuo.* (And with your spirit.)
> Priest: *Sursum corda.* (Lift up your hearts.)
> Server: *Habemus ad Dominum.* (We have lifted them up to the Lord.)
> Priest: *Gratias agamus Domino Deo nostro.* (Let us give thanks

to the Lord Our God.)
Server: *Dignum et justum est.* (It is right and just.)

19. Preface

At the chair at the foot of the dining room table (19), you saw your own priest's face to remind you of the Preface. This prayer changes during different liturgical seasons. The one in the missal booklet I use begins *"Vere dignum et justum..."* "It is truly meet and just..." We saw how in the New Mass (location 22) a variety of Preface Prayers are used in that form too. It serves to proclaim thanksgiving and praise to the Father, the Son, and the Holy Spirit.

20. Sanctus

Next, at the center of the dinner room table (20), was that freeze-dried coffee Sanka on a walrus' tusk. The sounds of the words "Sanka" and "tusk" will remind us of the *Sanctus*, and if you'd like to lock in the meaning as well, imagine that Sanka's written label thrice pays homage to God, calling him *"Sanctus, Sanctus, Sanctus,"* "Holy, Holy, Holy..." We saw this prayer in the New Mass at location 23 under the name of the preface acclamation, and here is what the priest acclaims (translated) in the Latin Mass. After the bells ring three times, the priest bows with hands joined, while all of the congregation kneels:

> Holy, Holy, Holy, Lord God of Hosts. Heaven and earth are full of Thy Glory. Hosanna in the highest. + Blessed is He Who cometh in the name of the Lord. Hosanna in the highest.

It is so fitting to proclaim "Hosanna," praise in the highest be to the

Lord in heaven, who is about to come join us on earth through the rites He gave us that immediately follow.

Before we proceed though, it's time to slow down a bit and see how we are progressing in writing anew the Old Mass on the tablets of our hearts. Please check the summary tables in chapters 6 and 7, along with the illustrations, or the master table in Appendix B. Do you have them all now, all of the first twenty parts? If you do, congratulations! You are almost half-way there! If not, why not rehearse until you have them locked in, ready to unlock the next time you attend Latin Mass?

Canon of the Mass

"Silence now reigns at the altar. In the Old Law the high priest alone entered into the Holy of holies. Like Moses, he spoke alone with God, and the Lord answered him. (Cf. Ex. 19, 10.) Thus, too, the priest recites in silence the wonderful prayers of the Canon, and renews the mysterious sacrifice of Christ's infinite love."
Rev. F. X. Lasance, *The New Roman Missal*[1]

On now to that wall thermometer (location 21) and peering inside you see (and hear) a most unusual scene. A British gentleman has just fired loudly a little toy *cannon.* He's apparently signaling his staff that it's tea time, because a servant immediately responds with great gusto, *"Tea, I get 'er!"* Back now to the seat on the right at the dining room table (22), and here we see again what appears to be a statue of the memory goddess *Mnemosyne,* but when you see her *toe* move, you figure she's really *alive!* On we go now to the head of the table (23) as we complete this chapter's briefest of memory tours. There you see Lenin, Stalin, Mao-Tse Tung, and Fidel Castro all trying to sit down in the chair as if in a game of musical chairs and the music has just stopped, and all the while they seem to be counting some objects on the table in front of them. So, to put it in a nutshell, our image here, believe it or not, needs to be *Communists counting.* Now let's get down to business and see what all of this means.

1 F. X. Lasance, *The New Roman Missal: In Latin and English* (Palmdale, CA: Christian Book Club of America, 1993), 86.

21. Thermometer	*Cannon blasts/"Tea, I get 'er!"*	Te Igitur
22. Seat on right	*Mnemosyne's toe moves*	Memento of the Living
23. Head of table	*Communists counting*	Communicantes

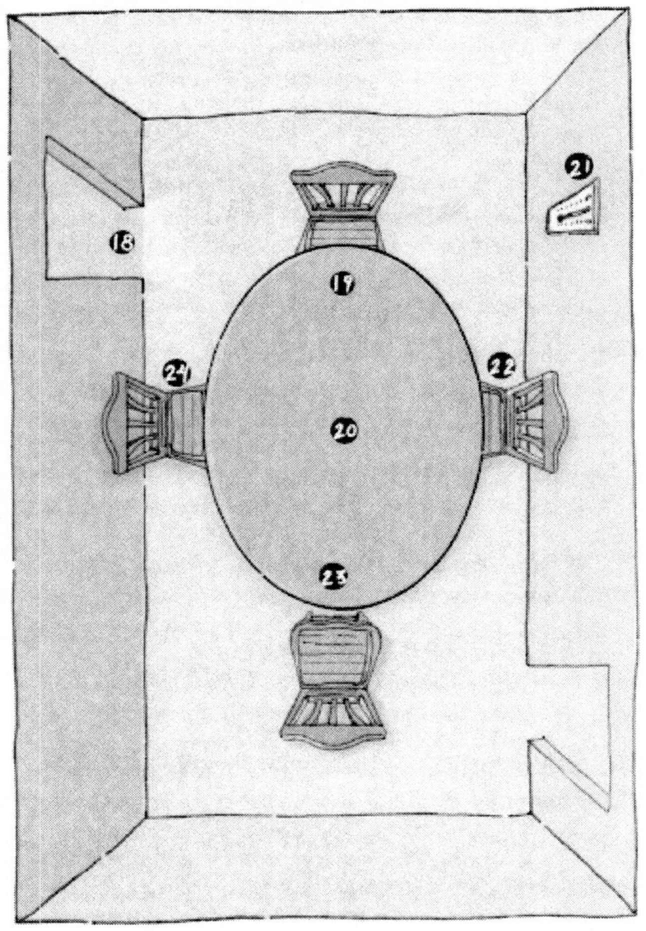

The Dining Room

21. Te Igitur

How come when we peered inside the wall thermometer (21) we heard a cannon blast and a British butler declare, "Tea, I'll get 'er!"? Well, of course to remind us of the Canon of the Mass and the prayer that begins, *"Te Igitur." Canon* is a Latin word meaning "a measure, standard, or rule," and in the context of the Mass, it begins with the prayer beginning *"Te Igitur"* (To You)[2] and concludes at the Communion Rite with the *Pater Noster* (Our Father). The holy prayers and actions of the Canon include the Prayers of Consecration, but to avoid an overly long chapter, for the lessons of memory are digested best in small servings, this chapter will include the Prayers before Consecration, and the next chapter the Prayers of Consecration themselves.

The *Te Igitur* begins, *"Te Igitur, clementissime Pater, per Jesum Christum Filium tuum, Dominum nostrum, supplices rogamus ac petimus..."* ("To You, most merciful Father, we humbly pray and beseech Thee, through Jesus Christ Thy Son, Our Lord...") This prayer is uttered

2 If you'd like to remember that *Te Igitur* begins this prayer with the first translated words of "To You," simply imagine that when the butler presents the tea, he simply says, "To you."

inaudibly by the priest while he bows before the altar. He asks God that our sacrifice to Him, through Christ, be acceptable and bring benefits of peace and unity to all within the Church, together with the pope and local bishop, and all who believe in the Catholic faith. It is preserved in the Ordinary Form of the Mass in Eucharistic Prayer 1.

The *Te Igitur* is so rich in meaning that throughout many centuries, it was considered most significant that the very letter "T" with which it begins, the *"Tau"* of ancient Hebrew, is the form of Christ's cross. Even in the Old Testament, Ezekiel (9:4-6) had written that God would save those with the mark of the *tau* on their foreheads. Observe your own copy of the missal for the Latin Mass, and you are very likely to see above the *Te Igitur* a pictorial depiction of Christ on the cross. In the days of "illuminated" or decorated books, the letter "T" itself of *Te Igitur* was often drawn as Christ upon the cross.

22. Memento of the Living

Next at the chair on the right (22), we observed the Greek goddess Mnemosyne, wiggling her toe, so we concluded she was living. Mnemosyne and the wiggling toe are simply there to help us remember the *Memento of the Living*. Next in the prayer before consecration the priest continues silently, *"Memento Domine, famulorum famularumque tuarum"* (Be mindful, O Lord, of Thy servants and handmaids…"). Here, the priest prays for the pope and bishop and all gathered at the Mass, declaring that the sacrifice is offered in praise of God, for the redemption of souls, and for the health and well-being of the faithful still living on earth.

23. Communicantes

Next, at the head of the table (23) we saw that unlikely scene of some infamous Communists counting something before them. Those Communists counting are simply there to remind us of the prayer that begins *"Communicantes."* Of course, no Communists are invoked in this prayer, but the holy communion of all the saints. Here, the priest silently begins, *"Communicantes, et memoriam venerantes, in primus gloriosae semper Virginis Mariae, Genetricis Dei et Domini nostri Jesu Christi...."* ("In Communion with, and honoring the memory in the first place of the glorious ever Virgin Mary Mother of our God and Lord Jesus Christ...") St. Joseph is next invoked, along with various apostles and martyrs who are specifically named, both from apostolic times and from the early centuries of the Church.[3]

Clearly, as we prepare for the mystery of the consecration, the Church Militant, those of us still on earth, by no means act alone, but in the company of the Church Triumphant, of the host of God's saints with Him in heaven. The priest asks God that through their merits and prayers we may be guarded and helped by His protection, through Christ our Lord. He concludes with *"Amen."*

Do you now know in order the parts of the Canon of the Prayers before Consecration? If not, it should take just a minute or two to peruse the table and picture and lock them all in. We've earned the brief respite this short chapter brings. In the next chapter we'll be taxed with ten parts of the Mass, those all-crucial prayers through which Christ Himself joins us at Mass in Body and Blood, soul and divinity.

---

3 They are Peter and Paul (named together as joint founders of the Church), Andrew, James, John, Thomas, James, Philip, Bartholomew, Matthew, Simon and Thaddeus, (Apostles) Linus, Cletus, Clement (all bishops of Rome ordained by Peter), Sixtus (Sixtus II, another early pope, whose deacon was St. Lawrence), Cornelius (an early martyred pope), Cyprian (martyred Bishop of Carthage in North Africa), Lawrence (martyred deacon), Chrysogonus (martyred under Emperor Diocletian), John and Paul (martyred under Emperor Julian the Apostate), and Cosmas and Damian (twin physicians martyred under Diocletian whose remains are in Rome).

Consecration Rites

"Hoc est enim corpus meum. Hoc est enim calix sanguinis mei."
Jesus Christ[1]

The seat on the left of the dining room table (24) conjures up a very moving scene (literally moving). The chair is transformed into the front seat of a car, and there you are as the passenger while Ichabod Crane is giving you a nighttime ride right through Sleepy Hollow. You see a good friend that both of you know, so you yell out, *"Honk, Ich. It's her!"* Now that makes a lot of sense, no? Well, we'll see in just a bit. We move now to the door of our family room (25). There just inside stands a *monk* holding up an *O*-shaped *plate* with an *"M"* on it. Something about his demeanor gives you some *qualms* about his intentions. Sitting upon the dresser (26) you are surprised to see a *priest* in the most ornate vestments you have ever seen. It occurs to you that he looks like Christ, and he's *raising a host* with a most striking look of *reverence and awe.* And also, just as he does so, you hear some bells ringing too. On next to the site of the television set (27), though in this ancient family room, it houses a rack of ancient scrolls instead. As you unroll a scroll, it bears an image of that same *priest*, now

1 See 1 Cor 11:24-25, Vulgate.

raising a chalice over his head with the same *reverence and awe,* and the same bells are ringing too.

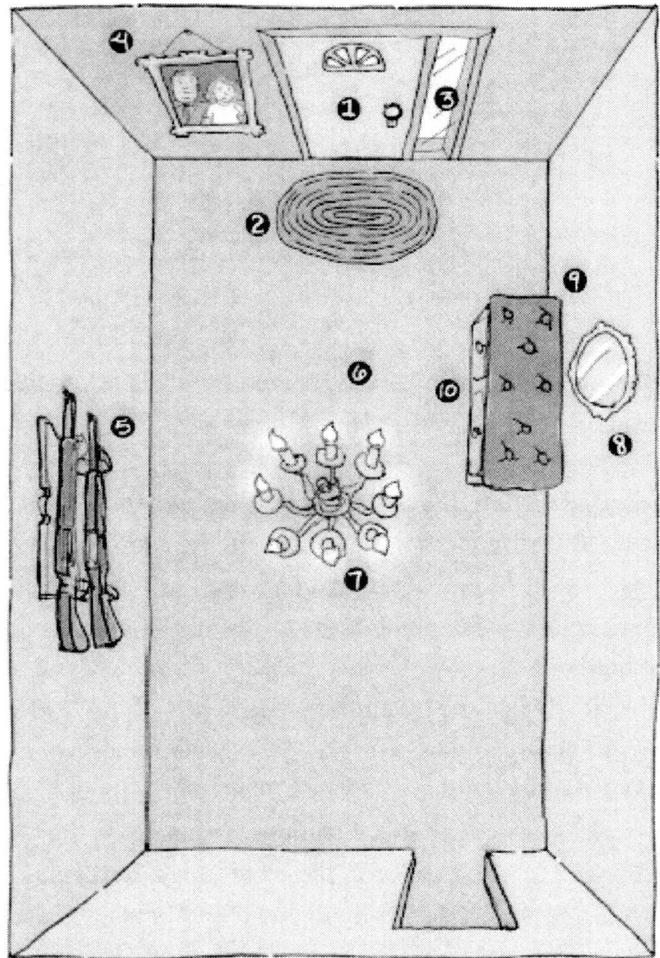

The Family Roon

Now you open up the closet (28), and on a stand rests a statue of *Mnemosyne,* but more striking by far is that *underneath* it is a statue of our *Lord, Jesus Christ.* Next we move to the weight bench (29), and who should be there all in blue, red, and yellow but *Superman* himself, bench-pressing the hugest barbell you've even seen, and he tells you that he'll show you the *proper way!*

Next we move on to the pool table[2] (30), where we see some *supplies* laid out for us—namely, *tea* and beef *Stroganoff.* Next to the pool table is that comfortable recliner (31), and here yet again is old *Mnemosyne.* This time though her toe does not move and neither does anything else. In fact, it appears she is *dead, and she is in a casket.*

Get ready for this next batch of images because it will take some explaining. Next to the recliner is the family room couch (32), and here we see a group of nobles, yelling out that they have just witnessed a powerful chest muscle (a pectoral) tear wide open a bus (perhaps it was Superman's pectoral!). The image you see then is *nobles quoting "Pec tore a bus!"* Taken back a bit by this room's most unusual scenery, you are relieved to see at the doorway (33) a most beautiful *Queen* who says to you, *"Hey, come near!"*

Let's see if we have this group of ten new images now, from 24 – 33.

24. Seat on left	*"Honk, Ich(abod). It's her!"*	Hanc Igitur
25. Door to family room	*Qualms about a monk with O-shaped plate with "M."*	Quam Oblationem
26. Dresser	*Priest in awe raises host, bells*	Consecration of the Host

2 We'll ignore for our purposes that games of billiards were not invented until the sixteenth century. For the purposes of this second memory tour, we'll simply make it a very old pool table!

27. Television (scrolls)	*Priest in awe raises chalice, bells*	Consecration of the Wine
28. Closet	*Under Mnemoysne is statue of the Lord*	Unde et Memores
29. Weight bench	*Superman shows proper way*	Supra Quae Propitio
30. Pool table	*Supplies: tea, stroganoff*	Supplices te Rogamus
31. Recliner	*Mnemosyne in casket*	Memento of the Dead
32. Couch	*Nobles quote, "Pec tore a bus!"*	Nobis Quoque Peccatoribus
33. Doorway out	*Per Queen, "Hey, come near!"*	Per Quem Haec Omnia

24. Hanc Igitur

Surely you won't forget that in the chair on the left (24) we saw that literally moving scene of Ichabod Crane driving you in a car through Sleepy Hollow. Seeing a friend you called out, "Honk, Ich. It's her!" That's simply because the first Prayer of Consecration begins with the Latin words, "Hanc Igitur," which literally means, "This, therefore," and which in the Mass is translated, "We therefore." To add meaning to our mnemonic image, you could imagine Ichabod Crane declaring that since you know that person, "*we therefore* honk at her!" To recall that during the Mass the bells are rung once at the commencement of the prayer, you could imagine the car horn sounds just like church bells. But now we must move to the true deeper meaning in the context of the Mass.

This prayer at the start of the Consecration Prayers announces the *oblation* (offering) of our sacrifice to God and pleads that it be accepted and that it wins for us peace in this world, freedom from damnation, and inclusion in God's holy flock. Dom Gueranger notes that the phrase in the middle—*"diesque nostros in tua pace disponas,"* ("Order our days in Thy peace,")—was first invoked by Pope St. Gregory the Great in the sixth century while the city of Rome was under military attack by the Lombards, and the words have been retained since, due not only to the great pope's holiness but also because, as reported by his Deacon John, at certain dire occasions, the Holy Spirit would descend in the form of a dove above Pope Gregory's head, whispering instructions about what to say into the pope's ear. The *Hanc Igitur* ends with the priest's words *"per Christum Domininum nostrum. Amen"* ("Through Christ our Lord, Amen.").

25. Qualm Oblationem

At the door to the family room (25) we had qualms about that monk with an O-shaped plate with an "M" on it simply to remind us of the sounds of the words *"Quam Oblationem."* Next, the priest begins to again bless the offerings, beginning, *"Qualm oblationem Tu, Deus, in omnibus, quaesumus, bene + dictam..."* ("Humbly we pray to Thee, O God, be pleased to make this same offering wholly blessed...") You can imagine the monk with the plate bowing humbly before God, asking that God approve our gifts and that they might be acceptable, becoming for us *"Cor + pus, et San + guis fiat dilectissimi Filii tui Domini nostri Jesu Christi"* ("the Body + and Blood + of Thy dearly beloved Son, our Lord Jesus Christ.").

26. Consecration of the Host

Atop the tall family room dresser (26) we saw a priest who looked like Christ, in the most ornate vestments, hold aloft the host with a look of reverence and awe. This image reminds us of the part of the Canon in which the host is actually consecrated. It begins, *"Qui pridie quam pateretur, accepit panem in santas ac venerabiles manus suas... "* ("Who, the day before He suffered, took bread into His Holy and venerable hands...") It concludes with the most powerful words of the priest in the person of Chirst, *"HOC EST ENIM CORPUS MEUM"* ("FOR THIS IS MY BODY"), echoing words of Christ Himself, at which time, through the power of God, the bread has indeed become sacramentally the body of our Lord Jesus Christ.[3] The priest then genuflects before Christ and adores the Holy Host as the servers ring the bells once. He stands up and elevates the host so that the congregation may venerate it, and the bells ring three times. He places the host on the corporal, genuflects in adoration one more time, and the bells ring once again.

What a sign of such deep reverence we see when, after having touched the consecrated host, the priest keeps his thumb and fingers joined until after Communion, except when he takes up the host. (Perhaps we should keep such reverence in mind, if we in the *Novus Ordo* should elect to take Communion by hand.)

27. Consecration of the Wine

At the site of what was first the small TV (27) and is now a small stack of scrolls, we saw the same priest holding aloft the chalice of wine, again hearing bells, to represent, of course, the consecration of the wine. The priest begins, *"Simili modo postquam coenatum est... "* ("In like manner, after he had supped..."), and then the priest recounts how Christ repeated the consecration of the wine in the chalice when it became his blood. He continues aloud, *"HIC EST ENIM CALIX SANGUINIS MEI... "* ("FOR THIS IS THE CHALICE OF MY BLOOD..."), continuing (in translation), "of the new and eternal testament: the mystery of faith: which shall

3 Again I refer you to Appendix C for a mnemonic consideration of the Real Presence of Christ in the Eucharist.

be shed for you and for many unto the remission of sins." Then the priest says quietly (in translation), "As often as ye shall do these things, ye shall do them in remembrance of Me." Next the priest genuflects and adores the Precious Blood of Christ. The servers ring the bells once. He stands again and elevates the chalice for the congregation, and the bells ring three times. He sets down the chalice, covers it, adores it in genuflection once more, and the bells ring once. The Body and Blood, soul and divinity, of our Lord Jesus Christ are now right before us and indeed will soon be within our own bodies and souls. Have we taken the time to consider the mystery, majesty, and astounding generosity of this sacrifice in which we are partaking?

28. Unde et Memores

Recall now that within the family room closet (28) we saw a statue of *Mnemosyne,* the old Greek goddess of memory, but underneath her was a more beautiful statue of our Lord, Jesus Christ. This was simply to remind us of the first words of the next prayer: *"Undes et memores, Domine"* (And now, O Lord…"). Christ told us to "do this in remembrance of me" (Luke 24:19; 1 Cor 11:24), and we are doing just that. The priest with hands extended prays in remembrance of Christ's Passion, Resurrection, and Ascension into heaven, recognizing that it is Christ the victim as well as the risen Christ whom we now glorify. Can we take a minute to let that sink in, that the glorified Christ is present before us?

The priest then joins his hands and makes the sign of the cross five times as he continues, *"hostiam + puram, hostiam + sanctam, hostiam + immaculatam, Panem + sanctum vitae aeternae, et Calicem + salutis perpetuae"* ("a Victim + which is pure, a Victim + which is holy, a Victim + which is spotless, the holy Bread + of life eternal, and the Chalice + of everlasting Salvation").

29. Supra Quae Propitio

As we moved to the inclined weight bench (29), we spied the mighty Superman bench-pressing the hugest barbell we'd ever seen and offering to show us the proper way. This is simply a reminder of the opening words of the next prayer, *"Supra Quae Propitio."* (To remember the word *quae* instead of way, you could perhaps imagine on Superman's chest, not a big "S" but a "Q!") Now back to the Mass itself. His hands extended, the priest begins, *"Supra quae propitio ac sereno vultu respicere digneris..."* ("Deign to look upon them with a favorable and gracious countenance...") The priest asks God to accept the sacrifice of the Mass as he did the sacrifices of the servant Abel, the Patriarch Abraham, and the high priest Melchizedek, all of which are described within the book of Genesis.

30. Supplices Te Rogamus

We saw that the pool table (30) was weighted down with supplies including tea and beef Stroganoff. The sounds of the words of this image are there to remind us of the infinitely more valuable supplies of eternal life which now lie upon the table of the altar. *"Supplices te rogamus, omnipotens Deus: jube haec perferri per manus sancti Angeli tui in sublime altare tuum..."* ("Humbly we beseech Thee, almighty God, to command that these, our offerings, be carried by the hands of Thy holy Angel to Thine Altar on high...") We might picture our supplies being carried to God by an angel to remind us of the meaning of these words and to remind us again that we are not alone at Mass but are joined by even the angels. The priest bowing down, his hands joined and upon the altar, he continues to ask through this prayer that we may share in every grace and heavenly blessing by partaking in Christ's Body and Blood.

31. Memento of the Dead

Upon the family room recliner (31) we saw *Mnemosyne* one final time, but this time within a casket. This image of Mnemosyne dead is simply to remind us of the beginning of the prayers after consecration, the Commemoration or *Memento of the Dead.* Standing, hands folded in prayer, the priest begins, *"Memento etiam, Domine... "* ("Be mindful, also O Lord...") and recites by name deceased "servants" and "handmaids" who *"dormiunt in somno pacis"* ("sleep the sleep of peace"). Here we pray for the Church Suffering, that the souls in purgatory will attain *"refrigerii, lucis et pacis"* (refreshment, light and peace). At this time we might also recall and pray for our own departed family and friends. As usual with so many of the prayers of the Canon, and because he presides in the person of Christ, the priest concludes: *"Per eundem Christum Dominum nostrum. Amen."* ("Through the same Christ our Lord. Amen.")

32. Nobis Quoque Peccatoribus

Upon the family room couch (32) we saw a sight that contends for the strangest of images in this memory house so full of the most unusual sights. We saw, you will recall, a group of nobles quoting "Pec tore a bus!" imagining that powerful chest muscles (perhaps those of Superman) tore open a bus (most likely to free people trapped inside). The image had to be so odd to suggest in English the Latin words that begin the next prayer, the *"Nobis Quoque Peccatoribus!"* Close enough? So now, what do those words mean?

Calling to mind the pectoral muscles,[4] it is with these first three words alone of all the Canon that the priest declares loudly as he strikes his chest,

4 The word *peccatoribus* means "sinners." It is the striking of the breast that actually touches upon those muscles of the chest.

"Nobis quoque peccatoribus famulis tuis, de multitudine miserationum tuarum sperantibus... " ("To us also Thy sinful servants, who put our trust in the multitude of Thy mercies...") He prays loudly and strikes his breast to declare himself a sinner, and then he invokes the intercession of a variety of apostles and martyrs, including some female sainted martyrs (Felicitas, Perpetua, Agatha, Lucy, Cecilia, and Anastasia) in expression of our hope that someday we might join them in heaven.

33. Per Quem Haec Omnia

The last location in the family room is the door on the way out (33), and here you'll recall we saw a queen proclaiming, *"Hey, come near!"* The Per Quem Haec Omnia begins, as you might expect by now, with the words *"Per Quem Haec Omnia"* and continues, *"Domine, semper bona creas, sancti+ficas, vivi+ficas, bene+dicis, et praestas nobis."* ("By whom, O Lord, Thou dost always create, sanctify +, quicken +, bless +, and bestow upon us all these good things.") If you'd like, you can imagine a Dachshund dog at her side, because this prayer precedes the Final Doxology. The priest now uncovers the chalice and genuflects. Rising, he grasps the Host in his right hand and the chalice in his left, performs the sign of the cross a full five times above the chalice as he recites, *"Per Ipsum, Et Cum Ip+so, Et In Ip+so, est tibi Deo Patri + omnipotenti, in unitate Spiritus + Sancti, omnis honor, et gloria."* ("Through Him +, And With Him +, and In Him + is unto Thee, God the Father + Almighty, in the unity of the Holy + Ghost, all honor and glory.") The priest then lays down the host, covers the chalice, genuflects, and says:

Priest: *Per omnia saecula saeculorum.* (World without end.)
Server: *Amen.*

So end the prayers of the Canon. We rise, and the priest recites that familiar prayer taught to his apostles by Jesus Christ Himself. The Communion Rite has begun, and we'll write it on the tablets of our hearts in the very next chapter. In the meanwhile, do you know the parts of the Canon? If not, let's look at the table and pictures until we know backward and forward all ten of its silent blasts.

Communion Rites

Facing the people with the Ciborium and holding up one of the Sacred Particles before the communicants the priest says:

Behold the Lamb of God: behold Him Who taketh away the sins of the world.

He then repeats the Domine non sum dignus three times as before his own communion, and going to the Communion rail places a consecrated Host in the mouth of each communicant, saying at the same time:

May the Body of Our Lord Jesus Christ keep thy soul unto life everlasting. Amen.

Fr. Lasance[1]

1 *The New Roman Missal*, 98.

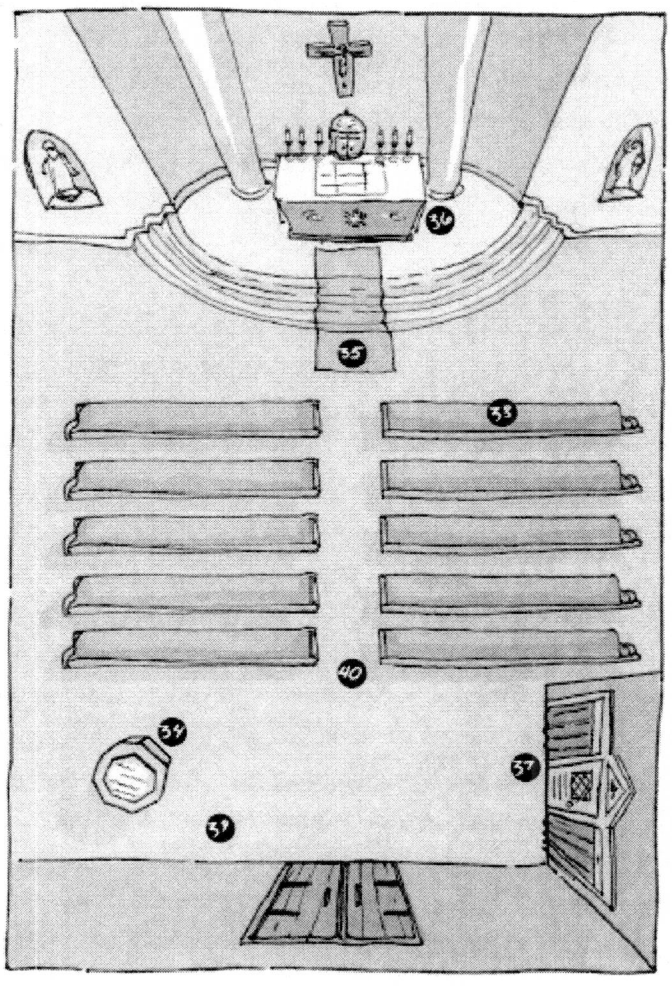

The Cathedral

We now enter a room of this house that we did not enter in our first tour, a room with not only a "cathedral ceiling" but, indeed, an entire cathedral! At the rear of the cathedral, right next to the baptismal font (location 34), believe it or not, you see a *potter* with his *nose* in a *toaster.* You can tell he is a potter by the clay on his hands. That toast must have just smelled a little too good, and now unfortunately, his nose is stuck. On next to the center aisle front (35), just before the steps to the altar, you see a famous *liberal* politician of your choice who says that he *knows* and then proceeds to *quiz us.* Next, at the site of the altar itself (36) you see a woman named *Agnes* holding up a very strange calendar with a big "X" on *"Day E."* Moving along to the confessional booth at the rear right (37) you *kneel in prayer*, your eyes fixated on a large *host* that is floating in front of the door. Stopping next (and the last time for this chapter), at the front right pew (38), you see *your priest consuming two halves of a host.*

That completes our memory tour for this chapter, and indeed we are only five locations from the end of our tour of this memory house housing the Traditional Latin Mass. Do you have them all backward and forward, inside and out: (34) at the font with the potter's nose in the toaster, (35) center front with the liberal who knows and quizzes us, (36) the altar with Agnes and her calendar's "Day E," (37) the confessional where you kneel in prayer before a host, and finally (38) the front right pew with your priest consuming two halves of a host? Sure you do! (If not, let's rehearse one more time.) Now that you've got it all, let's zoom in to see just what you have got.

34. Baptismal font	*Potter's nose in toaster*	Pater Noster (Our Father)
35. Center front	*Liberal knows/ quizzes us*	Libera Nos Quaesumus
36. Altar	*Agnes' calendar shows Day E*	Agnus Dei
37. Confessional	*Kneeling in prayer before host*	Prayers before Communion
38. Front right pew	*Priest receives two halves of host*	Communion

34. Pater Noster

How odd that within the baptismal font (34) we found a potter's nose stuck in a toaster. "Potter's nose, toaster" will serve to remind us through its sounds of the *Pater Noster.* To lock in the meaning of this image too, simply have the potter praying the Our Father! *Pater Noster,* of course, is Latin for *Our Father*. The *Pater Noster* is also known as the Lord's Prayer since Jesus taught it (Matt 6:11-19; Luke 11:2-4). This prayer has been part of the Mass from the early centuries of the Church. You already know the English words, and in Part I (location 24) we mused a bit on its meaning. For now, I'll present this prayer in Latin as it is said in the Mass (a beautiful and euphonious prayer well worth memorizing!).

First, the priest begins: *Oremus.* (Let us pray.)

Praeceptis salutaribus moniti, et divina institutione formati, audemus dicere:

(Admonished by Thy saving precepts and following thy divine instruction, we make bold to say:)

Pater Noster, qui es in caelis: Sanctificetur nomen tuum: Adveniat regnum tuum: Fiat voluntas tua, sicut in caelo, et in terra. Panem nostrum quotidianum da nobis hodie: Et dimmite nobis debita nostra, sicut et nos dimittimus debitoribus nostris. Et ne nos inducas in tentationem.

Server: *Sed libera nos a malo.*

Priest: *Amen.*

35. Libera Nos Quaesumus

At the center aisle of the church, before the altar steps (35), we saw a famous liberal politician (of your choice) who said he knows something and then proceeded to quiz us. "Liberal, knows, quiz us" will serve to remind us of *Libera Nos Quaesumus,* the prayer that follows and elaborates upon the last words of the *Pater Noster.* The Latin word *libera* here derives from the word for "freedom," *nos* means "us," and *quaesumus* means "to vouchsafe or give graciously." This prayer, familiar from a similar English rendering in the New Order of the Mass, begins *"Libera nos quaesumus, Domine, ab omnibus malis..."* ("Deliver us, Lord, we pray, from every evil...") As he recites this prayer, the priest holds the paten between his first and second fingers. The prayer includes a call for the intercession of the Virgin Mary, Mother of God, the Apostles Peter and Paul, as well as Andrew (Peter's younger brother) and all the saints, beseeching God that he might grant peace, help, mercy, and freedom from sin and insecurity.

The priest then uncovers the chalice, genuflects, and taking the host, breaks it in two pieces above the chalice, praying, *"Per eundem Dominum nostrum Jesum Christum Filium tuum..."* ("Through the same Jesus Christ, Thy Son our Lord...") He then breaks off a particle from the divided Host, saying, *"Qui tecum vivit et regnat in unitate Spiritus Sancti Deus."* ("Who liveth and reigneth with Thee in the unity of the Holy Ghost, God.") Then he prays, *"Per omnia saecula saeculorum"* ("World without end") to which the server responds, *"Amen."*

Now, the priest makes the sign of the cross over the chalice and says: *"Pax + Domini sit + semper vobis + cum."* ("May the peace + of the Lord be + always + with you.") The server responds, *"Et cum spiritu tuo."* ("And with thy spirit.") Here we see a difference in the two forms of the Mass, because there is no physical exchange of the sign of peace within the congregation. Rather, the priest then places the particle of the

Host in the chalice, saying quietly, *"Haec commixtio, et consecratio Corporis et Sanguinis Domini nostri Jesu Christi, fiat accipientibus nobis in vitam aeternam. Amen."* ("May this mingling and hallowing of the Body and Blood of our Lord Jesus Christ be for us who receive it a source of eternal life. Amen.")

As to why the Body and Blood of Christ are mingled, Dom Gueranger notes that the rite goes back over one thousand years and offers this interpretation of its meaning in words well worth pondering for how they remind us of just how intimately the Mass re-presents Christ's own sacrifice and triumph for us:

> Its object is to show, that, at the moment of our Lord's Resurrection, His Blood was reunited to His Body, by flowing again in His veins as before. It would not have sufficed if His soul alone had been reunited to His Body: His Blood must necessarily be so likewise, in order that the Lord might be whole and complete. Our Saviour, therefore, when rising, took back His Blood which was erstwhile spilled on Calvary, in the Praetorium, and in the Garden of Olives.[2]

36. Agnus Dei

Now you'll recall that upon the altar (36) we saw a woman named Agnes with an odd calendar open to a page showing "Day E." "Agnes, Day E," should serve pretty well to remind us of the *Agnus Dei,* and if you'd like to easily lock in the meaning as well, just have Agnes holding a lamb.[3] The *Angus Dei* in the old form of the Mass is the Lamb of God in the new form.

---

2 Dom Prosper Gueranger, *Explanation of the Prayers and Ceremonies of the Holy Mass,* 184.

3 My own parish is named in honor of St. Agnes. This early martyr (c.291–c. 304) is usually depicted holding a lamb in her arms.

The priest covers the chalice, genuflects, and then bows and strikes his breast three times in repentance of his sins. He then prays, recalling the words of St. John the Baptist:[4] *"Agnus Dei, qui tollis peccata mundi: miserere nobis. Agnus Dei, qui tollis peccata mundi: miserere nobis. Agnus Dei, qui tollis peccata mundi: dona nobis pacem."* ("Lamb of God, Who takest away the sins of the world, have mercy on us. Lamb of God, Who takest away the sins of the word, have mercy on us. Lamb of God, Who takest away the sins of the world, grant us peace.") Here we pray that the holy Eucharist will unite us all in peace.

37. Prayers before Communion

Our next stop in the mnemonic cathedral was the confession box (37), and as we knelt in prayer, to our surprise our eyes were riveted by a large host floating in the air in front of the doors. This image should remind us of the prayers before Communion. The priest directs his eyes toward the Sacrament and, not kneeling but bowing, begins the first of three silent prayers. The first begins, *"Domine Jesu Christe, qui dixti Apostolis tuis: Pacem relinquo vobis, pacem meam do vobis..."* ("O Lord, Jesus Christ, Who didst say to Thine Apostles: Peace I leave you, My peace I give you.") The remainder of this prayer asks God for peace and unity. The priest then continues with a second silent prayer for holiness directed to the Holy Trinity, beginning, *"Domine Jesu Christe, Fili Dei vivi..."* ("O Lord Jesus Christ, Son of the living God...") In his last of three prayers before his own Communion, the priest continues silently a prayer for grace, beginning, *"Perceptio Corporis tui, Domine Jesu Christe, quod ego indignus sumere praesumo..."* ("Let not the partaking of Thy Body, O Lord Jesus Christ, which I, though unworthy, presume to receive..."), and ending, *"Qui vivis et regnas cum Deo Patre in unitate*

---

4 The next day he saw Jesus coming toward him and said, "Behold the Lamb of God, who takes away the sins of the world" (John 1:29).

Spiritus Sancti Deus, per omnia saecula saeculorum. Amen." ("Who livest and reignest with God the Father, in the unity of the Holy Ghost, God, world without end. Amen.")

38. Communion

In the last location of this chapter's memory tour, we saw at the front right pew (38) your own priest giving himself Communion, receiving two halves of the host. This is because after the third of the Pre-Communion Prayers, the priest then genuflects, takes the host, and says prayers beginning with *"Panem caelestem accipiam, et nomen Domini invocabo."* ("I will take the Bread of Heaven, and will call upon the Name of the Lord.") Striking his breast, he utters those words recalling the centurion: *"Domine non sum dignus, ut intres sub tectum meum: sed tantum dic verbo, et sanabitur anima mea."* ("Lord, I am not worthy that Thou shouldst enter under my roof; but only say the word, and my soul shall be healed.") The bells are rung three times at the start of this prayer, and the priest repeats it three times. The priest then makes the sign of the cross over the paten, prays that the Body of Christ will give him everlasting life, and receives both halves of the host. He continues in silent prayers, praising and thanking God. Making the sign of the cross, while holding the chalice, he prays: *"Sanguis Domini nostri Jesu Christi custodiat animam meam in vitam aeternam. Amen."* ("May the Blood of Our Lord Jesus Christ preserve my soul unto everlasting life. Amen.") He then receives the Precious Blood of Christ.

The server then says the *Confiteor* (we encountered at location 2), and then the priest turns to the people and says, *"Misereatur vestri omnipotens Deus, et dismissis peccatis vestris, perducat vos ad vitam aeternam."* ("May Almighty God have mercy on you, forgive your sins, and bring you to everlasting life.") The server answers, *"Amen."* The priest then recites prayers in Latin including ones we encountered in the

New Mass's Invitation to Prayer (Part I; location 17) that begin *"Ecce Agnus Dei..."* ("Behold the Lamb of God...") and *"Domine, non sum dignus..."* ("Lord, I am not worthy...") In the Latin Mass though, bells are rung three times before the *"Domine, non sum dignus..."* and again, the priest recites this prayer three times.

And now it is time for us to receive the Lord Jesus Christ in Communion. The communicants proceed to the front of the church and kneel upon the altar rail. (In some churches without an altar rail the front pew may be used.) Kneeling, hands folded in prayer, the priest says, *"Corpus Domini nostri Jesu Christi custodiat animam tuam in vitam aeternam. Amen."* ("May the Body of Our Lord Jesus Christ preserve your soul unto life everlasting. Amen.") The priest places the host on our tongue, and we do not answer "Amen" but return to our pew in thankful prayer.

When all have received Communion, the priest returns to the altar, drinks wine poured into the chalice, and says prayers of thanksgiving, beginning, *"Quod ore sumpsimus, Domine, pura mente capiamus: et de munere temporali fiat nobis remedium sempiternum."* ("Grant, O Lord, that what we have taken with our mouth, we may receive with a pure mind; and that from a temporal gift it may become for us an everlasting remedy.") The rite of *ablutions* (cleansing) follows. Wine and water are poured into the chalice over the priest's fingers as he prays silently that Christ's Body and Blood that he has received will *"adhaereat visceribus meis"* ("cleave to my innermost parts"), removing any remaining stains of sins, refreshed by the holy Sacraments.

It would serve us to meditate upon the fact that we too have received Christ into our own viscera, our "innermost parts." Will we then do our part to show our gratitude in our actions for such a grand benefit?

The priest then recites a Communion verse from the epistle side of the altar (the right from our perspective). This prayer is a changing proper. The example from the Coalition in Support of Ecclesia Dei's *Latin-English Booklet Missal* is as follows:

Benedicimus Deum caeli, et coram omnibus viventibus confitebimur ei: quia fecit nobiscum misericordiam suam.

We bless the God of Heaven, and before all the living we will praise Him; because He hath shown His mercy to us.

Then from the middle of the altar is proclaimed.

Priest: *Dominus vobiscum.* (The Lord be with you.)
Server: *Et cum spiritu tuo.* (And with thy spirit.)
Priest: *Oremus.* (Let us pray.)

The prayer that then follows prepares us for the conclusion of the Mass and takes us into our last chapter. At this point, however, I pray that you do tell if you have memorized this chapter's five main parts of the Latin Mass, from the *Pater Noster* (34) to the *Libera Nos Quaesumus* (35), to the *Agnus Dei* (36), to the Prayers before Communion (37), to the Communion Rites (38). If not, it is time to rehearse them. If so, it is time to meditate deeply upon their meanings and to experience them when you next have a chance to participate in the most exquisite and extraordinary, Extraordinary Form of the Mass.

Post-Communion Rites

"It must surprise a stranger that, after we have solemnly told the people to go away, they stay and the service continues. The explanation, of course, is that the three elements after "Ite missa est," the Placeat Prayer, blessing, and last gospel, are all late additions....The Last Gospel is one of the latest additions to the Mass. The beginning of St. John's Gospel (i, 1-14) was the object of special devotion from the time of the Fathers. St. Augustine tells of a man who wanted this to be written in letters of gold in every church."

Fr. Adrian Fortescue[1]

On we go now to the back of our church (39), where you see a *stamped envelope* with the word "*Communion*" written on it. At the start of the center aisle (40), there stands not a bride getting ready to go forth, but a Japanese person, encouraging her friend Esther to eat some miso soup. You hear her say, *"Eat a miso, Est."* Now we move into our very last room where we need barely step inside to complete our whole memory tour of the Mass. You arrive at the door of a study (41), and on it is a

1 Adrian Fortescue, *The Mass: A Study of Roman Liturgy* (Middletown, DE: First Rate Publishers, 2015), ch. 10, section 3. Fr. Fortescue's book was originally published in 1912.

sign with an *old Irish blessing.*[2] Last, but certainly not least, sitting atop a small bookshelf just inside the door (42) is our familiar *"Good Newsboy"* proclaiming the best of news for the very *last* time.

The Study

2 I suggest this one: "May the road rise to meet you. May the wind be ever at your back. May the sun shine warm upon your face, and the rain fall soft upon your fields. And until we meet again, may God hold you in the palm of His hand." (You don't necessarily have to memorize it. Just enjoy it!)

Have you written this last batch of images on the tablet of your heart? If so, I must say, that's extraordinary! You have mastered all the key parts of the Extraordinary Form of the Holy Mass! This memory tour has ended. Go in peace to love and serve the Lord – but ideally not until you've considered the awesome significance of these last four rites of the Mass.

39. Back of church	*Envelope stamped "Communion"*	Postcommuion
40. Start of center aisle	*"Eat a miso, Est."*	Ite Missa Est
41. Study door	*Irish blessing posted on door*	The blessing
42. Short bookcase	*The last "Good News" boy*	The last Gospel

39. Postcommunion

We saw at the back of the memory church (39) an envelope stamped with the word "Communion." This image will remind us of the *Postcommunion* rites. The priest begins with a changing, proper prayer, such as this example, beginning with *"Proficiat nobis ad salutem corporis et animae, Domine Deus noster, hujus sacramenti susceptio; et sempiternae sanctae Trinitatis, ejusdemque individuae unitatis confessio."* ("May the reception of this Sacrament, O Lord our God, and the confession of the holy and eternal Trinity and of its undivided Unity, profit us to the salvation of body and soul...") The remainder of the prayer is the familiar phrasing declaring that this be through Jesus Christ in unity with the Holy Spirit, God for ever and ever, ending in "Amen."

40. Ite Missa Est

Back at the start of the nave's central aisle (40) we found that Japanese woman inviting her friend Esther to eat some miso soup, hoping that her English words "Eat a miso, Est!" would remind us of the important Latin words *"Ite Missa Est."* Having reminded us of the Communion we have just received, in the Postcommunion Prayer, the priest goes to the center of the altar, kisses it, turns to the people, and says out loud:

Priest: *Dominus vobiscum.* (The Lord be with you.)
Server: *Et cum spiritu tuo.* (And with thy spirit.)
Priest: *Ite, Missa est.* (Go, the Mass is ended.)
Server: *Deo gratias.* (Thanks be to God.)

This is the "Dismissal," and it is from the word *"Missa"* in the Dismissal that the Mass took its name. Still, at certain times, such as Lent, the *"Ite, Missa est"* is omitted and the priest instead faces the altar and says, *"Benedicamus Domino"* ("Let us bless the Lord"), and the server responds, *"Deo gratias."* ("Thanks be to God.") Dom Gueranger notes that it was expected that during the season of Lent the people would not leave the church right after Mass, but would stay for a time of additional prayer.

41. The Blessing

We just started to dip into the family room, and upon the entrance door (41) we saw that plaque with an old Irish blessing. The blessing here, though, is not Irish but Latin. The priest bows before the altar and silently prays a blessing, beginning, *"Placeat Tibi, Sancta Trinitas obsequium servitutis meae..."* (May the tribute of my homage be pleasing to Thee, O most holy Trinity...") The priest prays that the Mass be acceptable to God and bring forgiveness to him and to all for whom the Mass was offered, *"per Christum Dominum nostrum. Amen"* (through Christ our Lord. Amen.").

The priest then kisses the altar and turns toward the people, bestowing the final blessing:

Priest: *Benedicat Vos Omnipotens Deus, Pater, et Filius, + et Spiritus Sanctus.*

May Almighty God Bless You; the Father, the Son + and the Holy Ghost.

Server: *Amen.*

Dom Gueranger relates that because this blessing is a sign of joy, it is not included in *Requiem* (funeral) Masses.

42. The Last Gospel

At the last location of this memory house, sitting atop a small bookcase (42), was, for the last time, our most familiar *"Good newsboy."* We know well by now from past mnemonic experience, that the good news he proclaims is always the Gospel of our Lord Jesus Christ. Now this may seem odd to newcomers to the Old Latin Mass, that now another Gospel, indeed the same one every Mass, is proclaimed. The Gospel begins, *"In Principio erat Verbum, et Verbum erat apud Deum..."* ("In the Beginning was the Word, and the Word was with God, and the Word was God.") This is the first verse of St. John's Gospel, which makes crystal clear in the loftiest of words that the Lord Jesus Christ, about Whom he will tell us, was the Word (with a capital W) and verily God Himself. The reading proceeds through the end of the thirteenth verse, whereupon all genuflect as the priest declares from verse 14, *"ET VERBO CARO FACTUM EST"* (AND THE WORD WAS MADE FLESH") and (in translation) "and dwelt among us, and we saw His glory, the glory as of the Only-begotten of the Father, full of grace and truth." The server responds, *"Deo gratias..."* ("Thanks be to God.")

How strange, but beautiful and moving, that since the Middle Ages, when the Catholics of the time were so profoundly stirred by the words of the Word in this Gospel, the Latin Mass unto our time ends with this most sublime of Gospel passages.

This then, formally ends the Traditional Latin Mass, and yet if you attend such a Mass you will likely see that it is still not quite time to go home. Though it was omitted from the 1962 missal, Latin Masses will often conclude with the priest and congregation (while kneeling) praying in English the Hail Mary three times, the Hail Holy Queen, the prayer beginning, "O God, Our Refuge And Our Strength" (starting with the first verses of Psalm 46 [45] and adding calls for the intercessions of Mother Mary and all the saints), and finally the prayer to St. Michael the Archangel.[3]

There then, we have completed the entire memory tour of the Traditional Latin Mass or the Extraordinary Form. Do you have these last four parts down pat now, from the Postcommunion (39) to the *Ite Missa Est* (40), to the final blessing (41), and last but far from least, the last Gospel (42)? If not, you know by now that it simply means it is time for a bit more rehearsal. When you have them all down, why not set aside a minute for prayer to thank God and his Church for such a wonderful gift as the Roman Rite in not only one form but two! And now we'll move on to conclude with some thoughts on how we can more fully participate in either or both of these Rites, indeed, as if our life depended on it (because in a way, it sure does.)

---

3 Pope Leo XIII added this prayer to the end of the Low Mass in 1886. In my diocese of Springfield, IL, Bishop Thomas John Paprocki returned this prayer to the end of the *Novus Ordo* Mass a few years ago.

Conclusion: Full Participation at Mass in Heart, Mind, Body and Soul

"You shall love the Lord, your God, with all your heart, with all your soul, and with all your mind."
Matt 22:37

"Glorify God in your body."
1 Cor 6:20

Christ has called us to love God with all that we are, to give to Him all that we have to give. All that we have to give, our very existence itself, is of course a gift from God in the first place. He gives us his loving Holy Spirit too and his Son Incarnate, nowhere this side of heaven with such an immediate and intimate presence as at the Holy Sacrifice of the Mass. Whether performed in the Ordinary or Extraordinary Form, Christ gives Himself to us in his holy Word and in his Body and Blood, soul, and divinity. Christ is truly present to us at every Mass. As we sit, kneel, and stand in the pews, are we truly present to Him?

We are urged to actively participate in the Mass, in our physical presence and bodily actions, and in our hearts and minds too. Having worked to memorize the parts of the Mass, what can we do to become more present to Christ and to participate with Him more fully at every Mass we attend? Christ and His apostles have already advised us how to do so, by loving God with all that we are, in heart, mind, body, and soul.

Heart

The heart is at the heart of this book, since our goal has most clearly been to write the rites of the Mass upon the tablets of our hearts. Only important things are worth the concerted, repeated efforts of learning them by heart, and here the Mass more than qualifies. Important things are things that we cherish the most, things that affect the *core* of our being. The Latin word for heart is in fact the word *cor*, and metaphorically speaking, the heart is also the seat of love. When we make the repeated efforts to memorize the Mass, we demonstrate to God that the Son and His Mass are truly most dear to our hearts.

Mind

God made us in his image and likeness with intellect and will. Indeed, St. Augustine wrote that the three parts of the soul of *memory*, *understanding,* and *will* parallel within us the three persons of the Holy Trinity. God gave us minds or intellects capable of understanding in a manner far exceeding any other species on earth, and he expects us to use them, even, and perhaps especially at Mass. Truly the Mass is a mystery that exceeds our capacity to ever *fully* understand it, but Christ Himself has called us to love God with *all* of our mind. It is incumbent on us then to attempt to grow in the understanding of the Mass within the limits of our own mental powers. We will never begin to know those limits unless we strive to test them.

Let's think of that hour or so that we spend in the Mass. Do the parts of the Mass zoom by us one by one with only a vague sense of where we've been so far and what yet remains? Should we not rather strive to have an overarching understanding of the Mass's structure and sequence? Many of us move through Mass like the person who travels alone along an unfamiliar hilly road, never knowing for sure what lies beyond the next hill, when we could have the perspective of one who views the scene from above with a bird's-eye view, seeing the whole route and sequence of the Mass all at once, and grasping thereby how all the parts relate to each other like a great, holy symphony.

We use the reasoning and imaginative powers of our minds even as we memorize the Mass, for the memory methods we employ were invented through human reason and cannot operate within us without a great deal of thought and attention at first, until they become deeply ingrained and virtually automatic. Of course, since we seek not merely to *memorize* names and sequences of rites but to *understand* them as deeply as we are able, when we set this book aside, we will also pick up other books, the Scriptures themselves and other books on the Mass, books by great saints of all ages and by modern writers of our time who can take us ever deeper into the origins, development, and meaning of each and every part of the Mass, through the Scriptures and the Tradition of the Holy Catholic Church.[1]

Hopefully you have already begun to see as well that the very memory exercises within this book are a veritable workout for your mind as well. Decades of medical and psychological research has shown that to retain as best as possible one's mental powers of thinking, reasoning, and remembering as one ages, the golden rule that has emerged is simply "use it or lose it." Memory training is one way we can become stewards of the intellects God has graced us with, aiding us in maintaining the mental faculties God has given us as we inch closer to the likes of Methuselah.

Younger people too can profit through memory training in their abilities to love God with their minds. In our world of overwhelming technol-

1 The footnotes in this book can give you a start, since I have cited many, though not all of the excellent books on the Mass that I pulled from the great big box of dozens of books that has sat by my side throughout these months of writing.

ogy, many assume they need not memorize anything since the phone in their pocket seems to hold every answer to every possible question. Need the sequence of the rites of the Mass? Why not just do an Internet search? What a world of difference there is though from having the Mass accessible to you in an electronic gadget from having it written in the tablet of your own heart. When the Mass is in your heart and mind it can change lives for the better in a way all the electronic devices in your pocket or in the whole world can never begin to do.

That electronic world also provides us with a world of distractions, with temptations toward what medieval theologians called the vice of "*curiositas,*" that is of excessive caring and concern about things that do not matter. We see it today in electronic "addictions" for things like social media, Internet surfing, texting, and email checking, where people seem driven to spend hours at a time searching, skimming, clicking, and keyboarding, with each new message or image titillating but never satisfying, and with so very little worth resting upon and thoroughly digesting. These memory methods can help train us in the contrary virtue of "*studiositas*" (studiousness), which is the ability to focus and think calmly and deeply on the things that truly matter the most – like the Holy Mass.[2]

Body

God made us beings with bodies and souls, and our bodies are not unimportant.

We are to glorify God in our bodies by keeping our bodies sexually pure and by being good stewards of our God-given bodies through reasonable eating and exercise. Our bodies also serve to glorify God in the Holy Sacrifice of the Mass. Outsiders and newcomers to the Catholic Church are often perplexed by the various bodily postures and gestures that accompa-

2 See St. Thomas Aquinas's *Summa theologica*, II-II, q. 166 for his detailed treatment of the virtue of studiousness.

ny the rites of the Mass, and even many Catholics do not understand their complete significance, even in the New Mass. Whether standing at full attention, sitting to absorb Scriptural readings or a sermon, or kneeling in deep reverence during the Eucharistic prayer or at Communion, all of the bodily postures, including the bending of the knee in genuflections (*genu* is knee in Latin), bowing, and repeated signs of the cross are the visible demonstrations of our glorification of God at the Holy Mass. We should strive to learn the significance of each and every posture and gesture and to perform them with full understanding and reverence.

Soul

What better place than the Mass to reflect on the fact that God crafted us as ensouled beings with immaterial and immortal souls that will only attain complete and lasting bliss through the beatific vision of His Godhead in heaven. The Mass is a taste of heaven on earth. Christ makes Himself present, with all the angels and saints at his attendance. It is up to us to what extent we'll let Christ speak to our souls in the Liturgy of the Word and come and dwell and cleave "within our innermost parts" in the Liturgy of the Eucharist.

Admiral Denton, a prisoner on earth, called his time in prison a session in hell, and yet he was able to endure that hell year after year by his daily visits to heaven during which he mentally recited to himself the Mass, both in English and in Latin. May we learn from the admiral's admirable lesson what a thing worth cherishing is the holy and heavenly Mass. May we learn from the great Sts. Albert and Thomas Aquinas how we too can write the script of heavenly worship on the tablets of our hearts.

May we then strive to love God with all our heart, mind, body, and soul as we express to Him the deepest of thanks by memorizing the gift of the Mass, seeking to understand it more deeply, experience it more often, and live it more fully every day in every act of our lives.

Appendix A
Novus Ordo Mnemonic Master Table

LOCATION	*IMAGE(S)*	PART OF MASS
1. Front door	*Jubilant singers enter*	Entrance hymn
2. Doormat	*Mat signs cross and calls out "Greetings!"*	Greeting
3. Glass panel next to door	*Holy water sprinkler*	Rite for the blessing and sprinkling of holy water
4. Back wall next to door	*Baseball pennants*	Penitential rite
5. Gun rack	*Valkyries*	*Kyrie*
6. Center of foyer	*Singer or friend named Gloria (or "Old Glory")*	*Gloria*
7. Chandelier	*Collection basket full of prayers*	Collect
8. Mirror	*First-grade reader*	First reading

9. Bench	*Responsive palm tree*	Responsorial psalm
10. Drawer	*Second-grade reader*	Second reading
11. Center of living room	*Newsboy acclaims "Good news!"*	Gospel acclamation
12. Picture window	*Newsboy dyes a log*	Gospel dialogue
13. Sofa	*Newsboy reads Good newspaper*	Gospel reading
14. Coffee table	*Hominy*	Homily
15. Big-screen TV	*Professional fates*	Profession of Faith
16. Fireplace	*Universe within praying hands*	Universal Prayer
17. Living room doorway	*Gift-wrapped presents*	Presentation of Gifts
18. Dining room doorway	*Engraved invitation*	Invitation to Prayer
19. Foot of table	*Your priest prays over presents*	Prayer over the Offerings
20. Center of table	*Thanksgiving turkey dinner*	Eucharistic Prayer
21. Thermometer	*Face of priest/ dyes a log*	Preface Dialogue
22. Seat on right	*Your priest's face*	Preface
23. Head of table	*Your priest's face proclaiming*	Preface Acclamation

	Dove whispers into his ear	Epiclesis
	He holds host with crucifix	Institution/Consecration
	Mnemosyne next to him	Anamnesis
	Blessed Mary and saints	Intercessions
	Huge dachshund	Great Doxology
24. Seat on right	*Your father praying*	The Lord's Prayer (Our Father)
25. Doorway to family room	*Peace sign*	Sign of Peace
26. Dresser	*Lamb with halo*	Lamb of God
27. Television	*Invitation with broken host*	Invitation to Communion
28. Closet	*Altar rail*	Communion
29. Exercise bench	*You kneeling/praying*	Prayer after Communion
30. Pool Table	*Solomon makes sign of cross*	Solemn blessing
31. Recliner	*Teacher blesses your final exam*	Final blessing
32. Couch	*Army Sgt. bellows "Dismissed!"*	Dismissal

Appendix B
Traditional Latin Mass Mnemonic Master Table

LOCATION	*IMAGE*	PART OF MASS
1. Front door	*King David signs cross, says, "Adjudicate me!"*	Judica Me
2. Doormat	*Con fits Eeyore*	Confiteor
3. Glass panel next to door	*Cloud of incense*	Incensing the altar
4. Picture on wall	*Car made in Detroit, faded D*	Introit
5. Gun rack	*Valkyries*	*Kyrie*
6. Center of foyer	*Singer or friend named Gloria (or "Old Glory")*	*Gloria*
7. Chandelier	*Collection basket full of prayers*	Collect
8. Mirror	*Pistol with E rests on letter*	Epistle
9. Bench	*Graduate named Al goes up stairs*	Gradual

10. Drawer	*Al and Lulu on train track*	Alleluia or Tract
11. Center of living room	*Giant golden sequins trickle down*	Sequence
12. Picture window	*Newsboy proclaims "Good news!"*	Gospel
13. Sofa	*Fates in nice scene*	Credo (Profession of Faith/Nicene Creed)
14. Coffee table	*You offer Tory bread and wine*	Offertory
15. Television (scrolls)	*Cloud of incense rises*	Incensing altar, etc.
16. Fireplace	*Lava bowl for washing hands*	Lavabo
17. Living room doorway	*Sue, Skippy, & Santa eat a Trindad*	Suscipe, Sancta Trinitas
18. Dining room doorway	*Oar, latte, frat brothers*	Orate Fratres
19. Foot of table	*Your priest's face*	Preface
20. Center of table	*Sanka, tusk*	Sanctus
21. Thermometer	*Cannon blasts/"Tea, I get 'er."*	Te Igitur
22. Seat on right	*Mnemosyne's toe moves*	Memento of the Living
23. Head of table	*Communists counting*	Communicantes

24. Seat on left	*"Honk, Ich(abod). It's her!"*	Hanc Igitur
25. Door to family room	*Qualms about a monk with O-shaped plate with "M."*	Quam Oblationem
26. Dresser	*Priest in awe raises host, bells*	Consecration of the Host
27. Television (scrolls)	*Priest in awe raises chalice, bells*	Consecration of the Wine
28. Closet	*Under Mnemosyne is statue of the Lord*	Unde et Memores
29. Weight bench	*Superman shows proper way*	Supra Quae Propitio
30. Pool table	*Supplies: tea, stroganoff*	Supplices te Rogamus
31. Recliner	*Mnemosyne in casket*	Memento of the Dead
32. Couch	*Nobles quote, "Pec tore a bus!"*	Nobis Quoque Peccatoribus
33. Doorway out	*Per Queen, "Hey, come near!"*	Per Quem Haec Omnia
34. Baptismal font	*Potter's nose in toaster*	Pater Noster (Our Father)
35. Center front	*Liberal knows/ quizzes us*	Libera Nos Quaesumus
36. Altar	*Agnes' calendar shows Day E*	Agnus Dei
37. Confessional	*Kneeling in prayer before host*	Prayers before Communion
38. Front right pew	*Priest receives two halves of host*	Communion

39. Back of church	*Envelope stamped "Communion"*	Postcommuion
40. Start of center aisle	*"Eat a miso, Est."*	Ite Missa Est
41. Study door	*Irish blessing posted on door*	The blessing
42. Short bookcase	*The last "Good News" boy*	The last Gospel

Appendix C
Real Flesh and Real Blood: Christ's Real Presence in the Eucharist

Look! upon the altar lies,
hidden deep from human eyes,
bread of angels from the skies,
made the food of mortal man.
St. Thomas Aquinas, *Lauda Sion Salvatorem*[1]

By the consecration the transubstantiation of the bread and wine into the Body and Blood of Christ is brought about. Under the consecrated species of bread and wine Christ himself, living and glorious, is present in a true, real, and substantial manner: his Body and his Blood, with his soul and his divinity.
Catechism of the Catholic Church (1413)

For my flesh is food indeed, and my blood is drink indeed. He who eats my flesh and drinks my blood abides in me, and I in him.
John 6:55-56.

1 "Praise, O Sion, thy Saviour." Cited in Paul Murray, *Aquinas at Prayer: The Bible, Mysticism and Poetry* (London: Bloomsbury, 2013), 234. St. Thomas's sonorous original Latin text is as follows: *"Ecce, panis Angelorum, factus cibus viatorum, vere panis filiorum, non mittendus canibus."*

Sometimes things that are true can be very hard to believe. Try this one on for size: For about fifteen hundred years, virtually all of Christianity held an extremely important belief based on the unambiguous words of Christ himself. Then, in the early 1500s, a small group of men, disgruntled with abuses they saw within the Catholic Church of their day, proceeded to challenge, change, and eventually discard this belief (among others). Today, their spiritual descendants in the vast majority of the tens of thousands of denominations share their denial of the belief, though it remains the nearly two-thousand-year-old doctrine of not only the Roman Catholic Church, but also of the Greek and Russian Orthodox Churches and the Coptic, Syrian, Chaldean, and Armenian Churches, indeed, of all non-Protestant Christian bodies that separated from the Church before the Reformation.

Now, add to this odd story data from some polls from the late twentieth century that suggested as many as 38% of American *Catholics* do *not* hold this belief, and of those who do, as many as 70% do so in a confused and inaccurate way.[2] Whew! Hard to believe, huh? And what is this belief that so many find hard to believe? It is the belief in Christ's Real Presence in the Eucharist, of course, the subject of this hopefully most memorable appendix.

The *Catechism of the Catholic Church* teaches that the Eucharist is the "source and summit of the Christian life" (1324), "the culmination both of God's action sanctifying the world in Christ and of the worship men offer to Christ and through him to the Father in the Holy Spirit" (1325). Indeed, "the Eucharist is the sum and summary of our faith" (1327). Adding to the irony of those who reject this ultimate gift of Christ is that the ingratitude it reflects runs counter to the very meaning of the Greek word *eucharistein*, which is an action of gratitude and thanksgiving. We have so much for which to be thankful to God, most especially the gift of himself in his Body and Blood, soul and divinity within the blessed sacrament of the consecrated host.

Here we will examine the reasons why we believe this most glorious gift to be most undoubtedly true, especially since, as St. Thomas Aquinas

2 Gallup 1992 "Catholics Speak Out" Survey, as cited in Michael Wrenn and Kenneth D. Whitehead, *Flawed Expectations: The Reception of the Catechism of the Catholic Church* (San Francisco: Ignatius, 2006), 70, and Frank Chacon and Jim Burnham, *Beginning Apologetics 3: How to Explain and Defend the Real Presence of Christ in the Eucharist* (Farmington, NM: San Juan Catholic Seminars, 2008), 8.

has eloquently stated about truths of the faith in general, "the argument from authority based on human reason is the weakest, yet the argument from authority based on divine revelation is the strongest."[3] Indeed, as you will soon see, the strongest of all arguments in this chapter come from the very words of Christ himself. We will examine these reasons and all of their sources as well, from the prefigurements of Christ's real presence in the Eucharist in the inspired books of the Old Testament, to the words of Jesus Christ, his own apostles, and the Apostolic Fathers taught by those apostles and by all of the later Church Fathers, Doctors, and saints of the Church. We will lock in ten key reasons (from among many possible others), as well as their sources, be they Scriptural or from the great deposit of Church Tradition. We will examine them further too, employing our powers of reason to better understand the reasons for the faith that we hold in Christ's Real Presence in every celebration of the holy Eucharist.

Before we get down to the business of memorization and meditation on all of the reasons' profound implications, let's lay them out in a nutshell:

Ten Reasons in a Nutshell[4]

1. Christ's real presence in the Eucharist was prefigured by the bread and the wine of the priest Melchizedek.
2. Christ's real presence in the Eucharist was prefigured by the sacrifice and consumption of the Paschal lamb.
3. Christ's real presence in the Eucharist was prefigured by the manna from heaven God supplied to the Israelites.
4. Christ himself promised to provide his real presence in the Eucharist.
5. Christ himself delivered on his promise and gave his body and blood when he instituted the Eucharist.
6. Christ did not elaborate on his wording to explain that he was speaking only figuratively.
7. The metaphorical phrases "to eat flesh" and "drink blood" are used

3 *Summa theologica*, I-I, q. 1, a. 8.

4 Or, most literally, in a consecrated host. For an excellent recent book examining in-depth many more biblical reasons behind the belief in the Real Presence, see Thomas J. Nash's *The Biblical Roots of the Mass* (Manchester, NH: Sophia Institute Press, 2015).

pejoratively elsewhere in Scripture.

8. St. Paul echoed the words of the Eucharistic institution and pronounced it a grave sin to receive Christ's body and blood in an unworthy manner.
9. The earliest Apostolic Fathers proclaimed the real presence in the Eucharist.
10. All of the subsequent Church Fathers and Church Doctors have proclaimed the real presence.

Got the gist of them? Good. Now let's prepare not just to memorize those bare-bone statements but also to flesh them out fully and bring them to life, because as Christ told us, his flesh is real food indeed, and along with the drink that is his blood, it nourishes us unto eternal life.

Welcome to the Sanctuary of the Blessed Sacrament!

It is most fitting that to remember this most blessed of all holy sacraments, we will use as our system of mnemonic locations the sanctuary of our mnemonic cathedral,[5] because this is where the blessed sacrament itself takes place, as the priest, acting through Christ, consecrates the bread and the wine that become for us Christ himself, present sacramentally in his Body, Blood, soul, and divinity. The cathedral itself we will remember as the Cathedral of the Blessed Sacrament. We are blessed to have a Church of the Blessed Sacrament in my own town. Recently refurbished, the church is a beautiful sight to behold (and it is indeed one of the two churches in town in which both forms of the Mass are regularly celebrated). Well, now it is time to furbish our own mnemonic Blessed Sacrament Church with some astounding imaginary artwork that points to even more astounding truths.

Imagine now that you have entered the nave of the mnemonic Cathedral of the Blessed Sacrament and you respectfully approach its glorious sanctuary. Oddly enough, as you stand before the altar rail on the left (location 1), your knees begin to wobble as you realize that the floor is actually the *deck* of a ship and someone is swabbing the deck with *milk*. Odder still, loaves of *bread* and bottles of fine *wine* are strewn all over the

---

5 This memory cathedral was introduced in my book *Memorize the Reasons!*

deck. (Got all that – the milky deck with the bread and the wine?) All right, now our attention will move to the lectern (location 2), where you see a white *lamb* that is bleating at you! Moving along to the site of the liturgical book (location 3) sitting atop the lectern, as you try to read the first reading of the Mass the pages are obscured by *white flakes* of some kind that are falling fast on top of the pages. It's almost as if it were snowing inside.

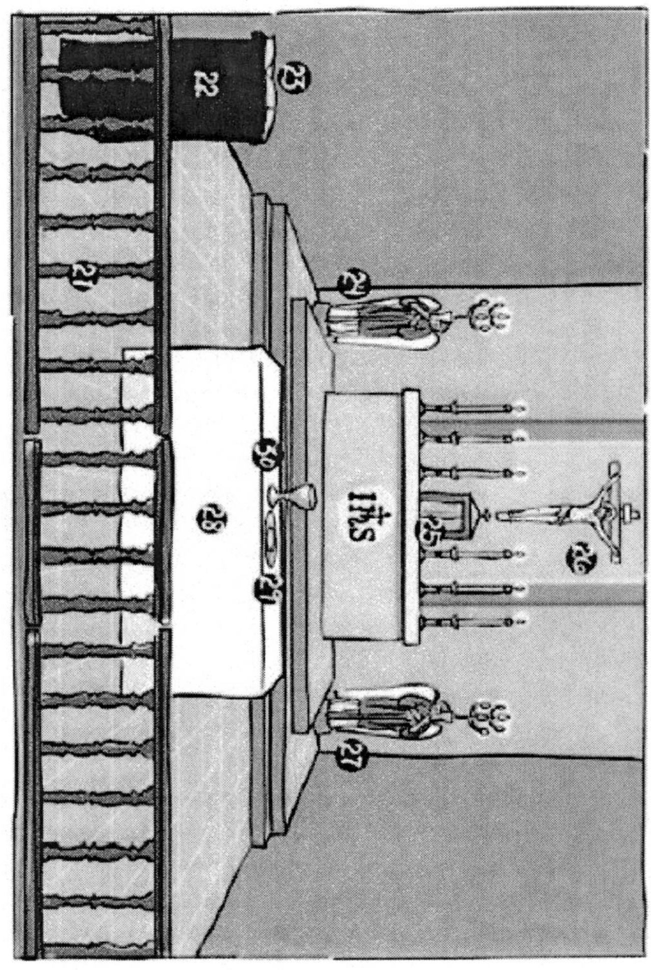

The Altar

Next we move to the angel on the left (from our perspective) of the high altar (location 4). With the angel are *Jesus* and a group of *disciples*. Jesus makes them a *promise*, at which they look aghast and *several of them leave*. Our fifth location is the tabernacle (location 5), and here is *Jesus again*, this time with his twelve apostles, *speaking grave words* as he holds up *bread* and *wine*. Above the tabernacle is a great crucifix (location 6), and *Christ* is upon it, surrounded again by disciples. You are surprised to hear them ask him about some kind of riddle and more surprised still when *Christ, though in agony, explains* it to them. Beside the crucifix is an angel on the right (location 7), and you see a shocking scene where *cannibals* are *eating human flesh* and *drinking human blood.* In fact, bizarre as this may seem, they are consuming *each other*.

Our last section of the sanctuary is the site of the low altar area, and upon the front of the altar (location 8) you see the dusty, bearded image of *St. Paul* stretching forward his left hand as if to say, *"Halt!"* and holding a sign in his right hand that boldly states, *"Warning!"* Upon the altar sits a shining, golden paten (location 9), and as is fitting, a consecrated *host* sits upon it. You admire the perfect host and are surprised when a *doctor* by your side (you can tell by the lab coat and stethoscope) asks you if you see the *seam* down the middle of it. Finally, we come to a beautiful *chalice* (location 10), and when it is raised by a priest, you hear the most beautiful bells, but you are again surprised when that man by your side asks if you hear the *clashing of cymbals*.

Okay then, there is the first little tour of the sanctuary that carries the seeds of images that will grow into tall oaks of memory and understanding before this brief memory tour is finished. Do you have each and every one of them down pat? Can you name all ten locations and images, from 1 to 10, and better yet, from 10 to 1? If not, then it's practice time. I'll lay them out now for easy review.

LOCATION	**IMAGE**
1. Altar rail on the left	*Milky deck with bread and wine*
2. Lectern	*Bleating lamb*
3. Liturgical book on lectern	*Pages covered with white snow-like flakes*

4. Angel on left	*Jesus makes promise and disciples leave*
5. Tabernacle	*Jesus speaks over bread and wine*
6. Crucifix	*Jesus, in agony, explains riddle to his disciples*
7. Angel on right	*Cannibals eat and drink own flesh and blood*
8. Front of low altar	*St. Paul holds a "Warning!" sign*
9. Paten on altar	*Doctor asks if you see the seam*
10. Chalice on altar	*Man asks if you hear cymbals clash*

Now that you have them locked in, it is almost time to provide the key to their meanings, but first we must lock in the sources of the reasons. Let's get ready then for another run-through, as we lock in four reasons from the Old Testament and five from the New, along with a couple from the Church Fathers, too.

The Sources Supporting the Sanctuary of the Real Presence of Christ

As we move back up toward the altar rail (1) with the milky deck strewn with bread and wine, you realize that you are not alone and your good friend *Jen* and her *sister* are there with you. Moving on up to the lectern (2), you discern a lamb is bleating most vigorously because it's about to be slaughtered, and it tries to sprint toward a large neon *"Exit" sign.* Remember the white flakes obscuring the pages of the liturgical book (3)? Well, now you notice another *Exit sign* right over the book, and after the word *"Exit"* it includes, for some reason, a long list of *numbers*.

There at the angel on the left (4) we saw Jesus making a promise, upon which some of his own disciples ran away from him. Now we notice hovering over Christ's head and flapping its wings a huge and magnificent *eagle*. At the site of the tabernacle (5), Christ was speaking over the bread and wine with the rapt attention of his apostles. Here again we find winged creatures hovering over Christ's head – *not* an eagle this time, but a great *winged man*, a great *winged lion*, and a great *winged ox* as well. Up on the crucifix (6), you'll recall that the suffering Christ explained some kind of riddle that his disciples had posed to him. Now you note that the great *winged man* from the tabernacle is hovering above and watching over Christ. At the angel on the right (7), we saw the most horrible scene of bloodthirsty cannibals sating themselves upon each other's human flesh and blood. Now you hear a man say to you in a strong British accent, "*I say* old man, do they know what you are eating?"

At the front of the low altar (8) was a foreboding St. Paul with his *"Warning!" sign*. You notice now that the path to the altar becomes completely blocked when from the ground emerges one massive *Corinthian column*. Upon the host on the paten (9) a doctor had asked if you saw the host's seam, though it looked completely whole to your eyes. Now you see that a cold *torch* he was holding has suddenly *ignited in flames*. Our last location was the chalice (10) that soon would contain Christ's blood. At the priest's consecration you heard pealing bells, but the man next to you said he heard clashing cymbals. Now you are surprised to be joined by a boisterous President *Theodore Roosevelt*, who tells you he must *mop* some *suet* (hard, white animal fat) from the floor.

Do you have the source images now, along with the images for the reasons? If you are not sure, it's time to rehearse them a time or two. Surely you haven't forgotten our lessons from good St. Thomas that the four things required to perfect a person's memory are as follows: 1) images, 2) an ordering system, 3) concentration, and 4) last, but not least, *repetition*. *"Repetitio est mater memoriae!"* he said – "Repetition is the mother of memory!"

Now, let's lay all this material out on this table before we dig deeply into just what it all means.

On Christ's Real Presence: The Words Behind the Word and His Reasons

LOCATION	IMAGES	SOURCE
1. Altar rail on the left	*Milky deck with bread and wine* *Jen and sis*	Melchizedek, King of Salem and high priest of God brought out bread and wine before blessing Abram (Gen 14:18; Cf. Heb 6:20, 7:17)
2. Lectern	*Bleating lamb* *Exit sign*	The lives of the firstborn of Isra-el were saved by the blood and the flesh of a sacrifi-cial lamb (Exod 12: 1-20: Cf. John 1:29)
3. Liturgical book on lectern	*Pages covered with white snow-like flakes* *Exit sign with numbers*	God fed the Isra-elites with manna that rained down from heaven (Exod 16: 1-36; Num 11:6-9; Cf. John 6:41, 51)

4. Angel on left	*Jesus makes promise and disciples leave* *Hovering eagle*	Jesus promises his presence in the Eucharist and describes the faith it will take to believe it (John 6:35-69)
5. Tabernacle	*Jesus speaks over bread and wine* *Winged man, lion, and ox*	Jesus institutes the sacrament of the Eucharist at the Passover with the words of consecration (Matt 26:26-29: Mark 14:22-25: Luke 22:1919-20)
6. Crucifix	*Jesus, in agony, explains riddle to his disciples* *Winged man hovers above*	Jesus explained to his disciples when he spoke metaphorically about bread and they did not understand (Matt 16:5-12)
7. Angel on right	*Cannibals eat and drink own flesh and blood* *British man says, "I say..."*	Isaiah relates the Lord and Savior will say he will make oppressors eat their own flesh and drink their own blood (Isa 49: 26; Cf. John 6:52-58)

8. Front of low altar	*St. Paul holds a "Warning!" sign* *Corinthian column*	St. Paul repeats Christ's words of consecration and warns of the judgment to come for those "guilty of profaning the body and blood of the Lord" (1 Cor 11:23-33)
9. Paten on altar	*Doctor asks if you see the seam* *Torch ignites in flame*	St. Ignatius of Antioch writes that the Docetists err "because they do not confess that the Eucharist is the flesh of our Savior, Jesus Christ" (*Letter to the Smyrnaeans*, 7:1)
10. Chalice on altar	*Man asks if you hear cymbals clash* *Theodore Roosevelt mops suet*	Theodore of Mopsuestia writes that when Christ "gave the bread he did not say, 'This is the symbol of my body,' but, 'This is my body'" (*Catechetical Homilies*, 5:1)

Christ's Presence in the Eucharist: The Meanings behind the Words Locations 1-3: Old Testament Prefigurements

So, why on earth, at location 1, the altar rail, did you find yourself (and your friend Jen and her sister) standing on a milky deck, strewn with bread and wine bottles? Well, to help you recall a very ancient reason for a very heavenly fact. In the very first book of the Bible, Genesis (hence our image of Jen and her sis), we are told the story not of a milky deck but of Melchizedek, the king and "priest of God Most High" (Gen. 14:18) who offered Abram bread and wine before he blessed him in God's name. Melchizedek was a prefigurement or foreshadowing of the ultimate priest-king, Jesus Christ, as is made crystal clear in the New Testament book of Hebrews 6:20, which notes that Jesus had become "a high priest for ever after the order of Melchizedek." The priest-king Jesus Christ, of course, was not merely a priest *of* God Most High, but God Most High *himself*. The bread and wine he would offer us would far exceed in substance the bread and wine offered by Melchizedek, and the blessing it would provide, as we'll soon see in Christ's own words, would be the very means to eternal life.

Next, at the lectern (location) 2, we saw that bleating lamb bolting for the Exit sign in fear of being slaughtered, to remind us of this scene from the book of Exodus 12:1-20 in which the Lord instructed each household of the Israelites to sacrifice a lamb. Its blood would save their firstborn, and its flesh would nourish them as God led them out of Egypt toward the Promised Land. They were to remember their deliverance in future times with "the feast of unleavened bread" (Exod 12:17). In the New Testament we find that Christ, the "Lamb of God, who takes away the sin of the world" (John 1:29), "our paschal lamb [who] would be sacrificed" (1 Cor 5:7), "a lamb without blemish or spot" (1 Pet 1:19), at the Last Supper has fulfilled the Passover sacrifice, saved our souls, and opened the way to heaven by the sacrifice of his own body and blood. (And of course, this is why in Mass we proclaim the "Lamb of God" [or the *"Agnus Dei"*] who takes away the sins of the world.)

A third Old Testament prefigurement of Christ's real presence in the Eucharist is found at location three. Surely you'll recall that the book on the lectern was covered with snow and above it was another Exit sign that also included a long list of numbers. The Exit sign and numbers are straightforward reminders of the books of Exodus and Numbers where the "snow" is explained. As for the snow, when the people of Israel grew famished in the wilderness and started to murmur against Moses, their leader, they woke the next morning to find "on the face of the wilderness a fine, flake-like thing, fine as the hoarfrost on the ground" (Exod 16:14). When they asked Moses what it was, he said, "It is the bread which the Lord has given you to eat" (Exod 16:15). *How interesting that like the Eucharist it prefigured, the Israelites did not recognize what the manna was by its appearance alone.* How striking that Christ himself would compare himself to that manna:

> Jesus then said to them: "Truly, truly, I say to you, it was not Moses who gave you the bread from heaven; my Father gives you the true bread from heaven. For the bread of God is that which comes down from heaven and gives life to the world." They said to him, "Lord, give us this bread always." Jesus said

to them, "I am the bread of life; he who comes to me shall not hunger, and he who believes in me shall never thirst" (John 6:32-35).

Location 4: Christ's Promise of the Real Eucharist

We've had a brief look at the Eucharist's foreshadowing in three prefigurements related in the Old Testament, but those hints were mere appetizers preceding the glorious feast that Christ himself would provide. At the site of our angel on the left (location four), you will recall that Christ had promised something to his disciples that led to some of them running away from him, as a great eagle flapped its wings over his head. Our eagle tells us this scene and the reason, come from the Gospel of St. John.[6] What Christ was promising them was the very subject matter of this chapter, his own Real Presence within the bread and wine of the Eucharist. These images are our reminders for the foundational Scriptural narrative in the sixth chapter of John's Gospel that underlies the Church's belief in the real presence. (I encourage you now, if possible, and later, if not, to thoughtfully read that chapter, especially verses 22-71.)

Let's first consider the *context* of Jesus' "bread of life" narrative. Recall that the day before Jesus spoke to the crowd at the synagogue in Capernaum, he had just miraculously fed thousands with five loaves and two fish. Moreover, twelve baskets were left over. The miraculous food that Christ supplied was without limit, a precursor to the miraculous manner in which he would feed billions across time with his own flesh and blood in an inexhaustible bounty. Christ prefaces this narrative as well by telling us that we need *faith* to believe in him. *If we really have faith in God and believe he created all that is out of nothing, would we deny him the power of Christ's Real Presence in the Eucharist when Christ himself told us that it is so?*

Consider as well that Christ would provide a miracle *greater* than the manna from heaven, because those who ate the manna died, but those who

6 As was explained in my *Memorize the Reasons!*, our memory images for the four evangelists' Gospels are based on their traditional depictions as a winged man for St. Matthew, a winged lion for St. Mark, a winged ox for St. Luke, and an eagle for St. John, deriving from the four winged creatures described in the books of Ezekiel and Revelation.

eat his bread of life will not die but will have eternal life (John 6:48-50). To give us ordinary bread, serving as merely a symbol, would seem far *less* miraculous and generous than the real manna that rained down from heaven.

Now let's move on and consider *Christ's promise*. To briefly summarize, the day after Jesus had multiplied five loaves and two fish to feed a multitude, some sought him out again, desiring more sustenance, and he minced no words in addressing them. Christ told them, "Do not labor for the food which perishes, but for the food which endures to eternal life" (John 6:27).[7] He said the food that never perishes requires faith that he was sent by God. They asked Christ for a sign to aid in their belief and reminded him of the manna God provided the Jews in the wilderness [31]. He proceeded to tell them it is the bread of God from heaven that gives life [33], and then he boldly proclaimed: "I am the bread of life; he who comes to me shall not hunger, and he who believes in me shall never thirst" [35], and he also proclaimed that he had come down from heaven to do his Father's will. Jesus' claims led to murmuring among the crowd, and he chastised them for doing so, reiterating again and again[8] his clear and shocking message: "I am the bread of life" [48]; "I am the living bread which came down from heaven; if anyone eats[9] of this bread he will live forever and the bread which I shall give for the life of the world is my flesh" [51]; "unless you eat the flesh of the Son of man, you have no life in you; he who eats my flesh and drinks my blood has eternal life, and I will raise him up at the last day" [54]. "For my flesh is food indeed and my blood is drink indeed" [55].

---

7 The remaining numbers in brackets refer to the verse numbers in John 6.

8 Karl Keating has emphasized in his chapter on the Eucharist in *Catholicism and Fundamentalism: The Attack on "Romanism" by "Bible Christians" (*San Francisco: Ignatius Press, 1988), 234, that Jesus said he was the bread that came down from heaven a full *twelve* times, and that they would have "to eat my flesh and drink my blood" *four* times. (Clearly Jesus was aware of the power of repetition for emphasis, and indeed as well, that repetition is the mother of memory!)

9 The Greek word trogov (transliterated "trogon") is used for "eats" (John 6:57), which means to "gnaw," "bite," or "chew." This is not the language of a tame, symbolic figure of speech, but the blunt words of a "hard saying." Christ's words are hard to believe for many, and hard to understand for all. *How* Christ is present in the Eucharist is a great mystery that exceeds human understanding, but *that* he is really present was a united belief in the Christian world for more than fifteen hundred years.

These words and more he said as he taught in the synagogue in Capernaum, and his words were not well-taken by many. "Many of his disciples, when they heard it, said, 'This is a hard saying; who can listen to it?'" [60]. Jesus, though, did not soften his "hard" words. "After this, many of his disciples drew back and no longer went about with him" [(66]. That is why our image depicts some disciples running away from Christ. They were running away from the natural "flesh and blood" Christ, as many more, fifteen hundred years later, would run away from the sacramental "flesh and blood" Christ under the appearance of bread and wine in the Eucharist.

How ironic that many fundamentalists who attack the Church as unscriptural, reject Christ's clear words here and interpret this passage metaphorically, while *the Catholic Church takes the Word literally at his word!* We'll unpack more fully Christ's John 6 narrative as we proceed through additional reasons.

Location 5: Christ Institutes the Eucharist

We now move to location 5, that of the tabernacle, and here we saw Christ with his apostles, speaking over bread and wine, with a winged man, lion, and ox, all hovering above. How fitting that this holy place that holds the Eucharist will also hold the place where we recall just how Christ instituted the first Eucharist at the Last Supper. St. John, the eagle, told us of Christ's promise of the Eucharist, and his evangelist colleagues, Sts. Matthew (26: 26-30), Mark (14:22-26), and Luke (22:14-20), tell us just how he fulfilled that promise on the night he was betrayed. St. Paul would recount this fateful night as well (1 Cor 11: 23-25), so you may feel free to include an image of him here too – using perhaps the image of a friend of yours named Paul.

Here is the heart of the passage from Matthew 26:26-28:

> "Now as they were eating, Jesus took bread, and blessed, and broke it, and gave it to his disciples and said, 'Take, eat; this is my body.' And he took a cup, and when he had given thanks he gave it to them, saying, 'Drink of it, all of you; for this is my blood of the covenant, which is poured out for many for the forgiveness of sins.'"

The gist of these words, which ring so familiar to any who attend a Mass in our day and hear the Eucharistic Prayer, is provided with slight variance of wording, but identical meaning in all three Gospel accounts, as well as in St. Paul's rendering. Here was Christ, on what he knew was his last night before his Crucifixion, delivering in plain terms his last will and testament to his closest friends on earth. The Catholic Church does and has always taken him at his literal word. Christ says this "is" his body and blood, not that it "represents" or "symbolizes" them, as deniers of the real presence claim he meant. We will soon further examine the arguments of those who propose that it boils down to the matter, so to speak, of a most nuanced analysis of just what the meaning of "is" is.[10]

Locations 6-8: Fleshing Out Christ's Words through the Scriptures

In essence, the whole issue of Christ's Real Presence in the Eucharist does boil down to just what he meant in the passages in John 6, Matthew 26, Mark 14, Luke 22, and 1 Corinthians 11. His words, as we've seen, could hardly be more plain, direct, and emphatic, and yet so many modern Christians deny that he really meant what he said. It is through the context of Scripture as a whole, and through the written testimony of a myriad of early Christians, that many compelling arguments can be made to show, as the Council of Trent explicitly declared in response to the challenges of the Reformers in the sixteenth century, that Christ was *not* speaking *figuratively*. Indeed, as Christ himself said, "For my flesh is food indeed, and my blood is drink indeed" (John 6:55). Now let's make sure we've memorized and understood all the compelling supporting evidence.

At location six, the crucifix above the tabernacle, you'll recall that the apostles were asking Christ to explain some kind of riddle, as the great winged man hovered over him. Now, before explaining this riddle and Christ's explanation, I'll provide you a riddle, in the form of an image of an ordinary loaf of bread. Please imagine that the apostles are holding a modern, store-bought loaf of sliced bread and asking Christ to explain what it is. What could that bread mean?

10 The Greek word *esti* is appropriately translated in English as "is," since it is the third person singular of the word for "to be."

Okay, now I've got some explaining to do. The winged man, of course, tells us we are dealing with a passage from St. Matthew's Gospel (16:5-12) to be exact. Here, in another passage relating to bread, Jesus does speak metaphorically, telling his apostles, "Take heed and beware of the leaven of the Pharisees and Sadducees" [6]. They discuss it amongst themselves and tell Jesus, "We brought no bread" [7]. They had missed Jesus' point and took him literally when he had spoken figuratively, and what did Jesus do? He corrected their misunderstanding, and explained his true meaning explicitly. "How is it that you fail to perceive that I did not speak about bread? Beware of the leaven of the Pharisees and Sadducees" [11]. Then they understood that he did not tell them to beware of the actual leaven of bread, but of the teaching of the Pharisees and Sadducees.

The store-bought bread in our image simply reminds us that the subject of this passage was also bread, but ordinary bread, not the bread from heaven that is the body of Christ. Note well here Christ's response to his apostles' misunderstanding. *He elaborates and sets them straight when they interpret literally what he meant figuratively.* Indeed, Christ was the greatest of teachers, and this was his standard operating procedure![11] Christ sure does talk of himself in a figurative sense at times, as when he proclaims, "I am the true vine" (John 15:1) and "I am the door" (John 10:9). In fact, regarding his first reference to the "door" metaphor, John 10:6 expressly states: "This figure Jesus used with them, but they did not understand what he was saying to them." Note well the word "figure" (as in figure of speech), and note as well that because of the confusion, Jesus then proceeded to explain his meaning (John 10:7-18).

Now, let's consider in more depth what happened in the all-important discussion of bread in the John 6 narrative. Think about it. The crowd that was present at that synagogue in Capernaum heard Christ's own words *live*, complete with his own intonations, facial expressions, and bodily gestures, and there is no question but that they took him most *literally*. They murmured when he claimed to be the bread of life [41], and after he proclaimed the full discourse and the need to eat his flesh and drink his

11 In their *Beginning Apologetics 3: How to Explain and Defend the Real Presence of Christ in the Eucharist*, 12, Frank Chacon and Jim Burnham provide a helpful summary chart detailing six passages from the Gospels in which Christ corrects people when they *wrongly* take him literally (in addition to the Matthew 16 passage we examined), and three in which Christ confirms and repeats his statements when people *rightly* take him literally.

blood, many called it a "hard saying" [60], and many of his own disciples "drew back and no longer went about with him" [66]. Indeed, Jesus asked his own twelve disciples, and Peter in particular, if they too would leave him. This is when Peter uttered those hauntingly beautiful words, "Lord, to whom shall we go? You have the words of eternal life; and we have believed, and have come to know, that you are the Holy One of God" [68-69]. Jesus then mentioned one who did not believe him, not calling him by name, but describing him as "a devil" [70]. He spoke, in a sense, of *the first clear denier of Christ's Real Presence in the Eucharist, the apostle Judas Iscariot.*

If the crowd, Christ's disciples, and even his rock, Peter, had misinterpreted his words, taking as literal words he meant to be metaphorical, why did he not correct them this time? Why would he let people leave from him? Why would he let his Church fall into an error that would not be corrected for fifteen hundred years? Could it be presumptuous to think that we can better understand Christ's words across the centuries of time, despite translation of language, than did his own beloved apostles who stood with him face-to-face and saw his own lips shape his words that day?

On now to location 7. Here, at the site of our angel on the right, you saw that heinous scene of cannibals feasting on their own flesh and blood, and heard the man with a strong British accent exclaim, "I *say*, old man! Do you know what they're eating?" The first words of the Brit's exclamation are simply our sound-alike reminder that our passage comes from the book of Isaiah. Here is the verse: "I will make your oppressors eat their own flesh, and they shall be drunk with their own blood as with wine" (49:26). Now let's see what this all means.

Not only do deniers of the real presence interpret Christ's words that the bread and wine are his body and blood as only figurative, they argue the same about his words when he said repeatedly in John 6 that we must eat his flesh and drink his blood. Some argue too that Jesus himself explained that he was speaking figuratively in John 6:63: "It is the spirit that gives life, the flesh is of no avail; the words I have spoken to you are spirit and life."

Our image is intended to help us recall several reasons we should deny a figurative interpretation and once again affirm Christ's plain, literal words. First, and most directly, our self-consuming cannibals call to mind the horrible curse in Isaiah that the Jews' oppressors would be made to eat their own flesh and drink their own blood. In fact, the phrase to "eat the flesh" or "drink the blood" of someone was already a commonly used figure of speech, meaning to grievously harm someone. It appears with that meaning in at least six other places in both testaments of the Bible, for instance, from Psalm 27:2, "When evildoers assail me,"[12] to 2 Samuel 23:15-17 when David declared, "Shall I drink the blood of the men who went at the risk of their lives?" to Revelation 17:16: "they will make her desolate and naked, and devour her flesh and burn her up with fire." Clearly then, this "figure of speech" already had a very specific and very negative meaning to the crowd at the synagogue at Capernaum. This could not possibly be how Christ intended it.[13]

Further, as for Christ's words that "the flesh is of no avail" (John 6:63), note well that Christ refers to "*the* flesh" in this instance as carnal man without spiritual faith, and when he describes the Eucharist, he clearly states, "*my* flesh." There is a world of difference between "the" and "my" in those statements; the first, indeed a figural term (as St. Paul expounds in 1 Cor 2:14-15) in contrasting the "unspiritual" or "carnal" man of the flesh with the "spiritual" man, and the second, Christ's literal term for his own literal flesh, the same flesh that he would offer on the cross to win our salvation.

Speaking of St. Paul, on we go to the altar (location 8), as we saw him holding one hand out to motion us to "Halt!" while in the other hand, he held up a "Warning!" sign. Sprouting from the floor, right next to him, was a single Corinthian column. That column, of course, signals 1 Corinthians, and there St. Paul recounted Christ's words from the institution of the Eucharist. Now, let's listen to what he went on to warn us about:

> "Whoever, therefore, eats the bread or drinks the cup of the Lord in an unworthy manner will be guilty of the profaning of the body and blood of the Lord. Let a man examine himself, and so eat of the bread and drink of the cup. For anyone who eats and drinks without discerning the body eats and drinks judgment upon himself" (1 Cor 11: 27-29).

---

12 A footnote in the RSV explains "Heb [i.e., Hebrew] *to eat up my flesh*."

13 As Chacon and Burnham so elegantly state the *argument ad absurdum*, "If Jesus is speaking only figuratively about eating His flesh and drinking His blood, as many non-Catholics claim, then what He really means is *"whoever persecutes, assaults, and destroys Me will have eternal life!" Beginning Apologetics 3,* 14.

St. Paul, like Christ before him, spoke most plainly and forcefully about the Real Presence of Christ in the Eucharist. Why the stern warning and condemnation if he's talking about mere bread and wine? St. Paul explicitly expects followers of Christ to "discern"[14] the body and blood of the Lord in the Eucharistic elements of the bread and wine, so of course he must believe they are present for the discerning! That discerning, in turn, is for the "spiritual" person of faith St. Paul described in 1 Corinthians 3, since as Christ made clear in John 6, belief in his presence in the Eucharist requires not an act of bodily vision, or taste, but an act of *faith*.

Locations 9-10: The Real Presence in Christ's Church

We have seen from the reactions of the people who actually heard and witnessed Christ's "bread of life" narrative in John 6 that they clearly believed he was speaking literally about his body and blood, preaching a "hard saying" that led many to leave him. Now we turn to the early centuries of Christians who lived after the time of Christ but heard of his words from his own apostles or through those apostles' own disciples.

At location 9, the paten on the altar, you'll recall that a doctor asked you if you noticed a seam down the middle of a host. A torch he was holding then burst into flames. Now, a sudden ignition into flames will always tell us, of course, that St. Ignatius of Antioch is somewhere about! The image of the doctor is our reminder that he was writing about the error of the group called the Docetists who taught that Jesus only *seemed* to be truly human. Our images serve to remind us of these words of his that were directed toward the Docetists—those who were spreading unorthodox opinions, those who "deny the gift of God and are perishing in their disputes." Here are his words of guidance to the Christians living in Smyrna[15] regarding the Docetists: "They abstain from the Eucharist and from prayer, because they do not confess that the Eucharist is the Flesh of

14 The word "discerning" here is not unique to the RSV, and is found as well in the KJV, NIV, and many other versions. The vast majority of English translations use "discerning," and some use the similar "recognizing" or "distinguishing," though I've noticed that the NIV substitutes the word "honoring." The actual Greek word is " diakrinov" transliterated "diakrinon."

15 A coastal town in modern-day Turkey. This church was one of the seven addressed in Revelation 1:11 and 2: 8-11.

our Savior Jesus Christ, Flesh which suffered for our sins and which the Father, in His goodness, raised up again."[16]

St. Ignatius, *a student of the same St. John who penned the bread of life narrative,* clearly believed that Christ was truly present in the Eucharist, and that recognition of his presence was extremely important for the salvation of each believer and for the good of the Church. The flesh of the Eucharist, he makes plain as day, is the same flesh that suffered for us on the cross. In our image, the doctor asked if you saw the *seam* down the center of the host, to remind us again, that the true nature of the host is much *more than it seems* with the naked eye that lacks the light of faith in Christ's words. This too, was not the only time St. Ignatius wrote about the Real Presence. In his *Letter to the Romans*, for example, he wrote of his hunger and thirst for the body and blood of Christ. He knew that what appears to our eyes as bread and wine are much more than they seem.

Let's move along now, to our tenth and last location. St. Ignatius was the first but by no means the last of the ancient Church Fathers to express his clear belief that the consecrated bread and wine are the body and blood of the Savior, Jesus Christ. In his masterful summary of Catholic belief, Ludwig Ott cites seven pre-Nicene Fathers and seven post-Nicene Fathers who wrote about the Real Presence.[17] There were other Church Fathers who also spoke and wrote clearly on the Real Presence, and it is to one of them that we will turn next. Indeed, he's the reason President Theodore Roosevelt declared he must mop suet when you saw the chalice on the altar. Recall as well that when you heard the bells at the consecration, a man asked if you heard the clash of cymbals, and you'll have this whole reason down pat. Behold now the words of Theodore of Mopsuetta:

> It is proper, therefore, that when [Christ] gave the Bread He did not say, "This is the symbol of My Body," but, "This is My Body." In the same way when He gave the Cup He did not say,

---

16 William A. Jurgens, *The Faith of the Early Fathers* (Collegeville, MN: Liturgical Press), 1:25.

17 Ludwig Ott, *Fundamentals of Catholic Dogma* (Rockford, IL: TAN Books, 1974), 375-378. His pre-Nicene examples (prior to the first ecumenical council at Nicea in AD 325) are Sts. Ignatius of Antioch, Justin Martyr, Irenaeus of Lyons, Clement of Alexandria, and Cyprian, as well as Origen and Tertullian. His post-Nicene examples are Sts. Cyril of Jerusalem, John Chrysostom, Cyril of Alexandria, John of Damascus, Hilary of Poitiers, Ambrose, and Augustine.

> "This is the symbol of My Blood," but, "This is My Blood"; for He wanted us to look upon the [Eucharistic elements] after their reception of grace and the coming of the Holy Spirit not according to their nature, but [that we should] receive them as they are, the Body and Blood of our Lord. We ought...not regard the [Eucharistic elements] merely as bread and cup, but as the Body and Blood of Christ, into which they were transformed by the descent of the Holy Spirit.[18]

Theodore of Mopsuestia (AD 350-428) was a friend of the great Eastern Church Father and Church Doctor, St. John Chrysostom. On account of some questionable writings, Mopsuestia was at one point condemned of contributing to the ancient error of Nestorianism, which asserted a separation between the human and divine persons of Christ, though modern scholars doubt that he was truly guilty of that charge.[19] The reason I've selected his passage as the last of our reasons, among the many writings of the post-Nicene Fathers proclaiming the Real Presence, is that he so clearly states and refutes the argument of some Reformers that is so prevalent today: that the bread and wine of the Eucharist are mere *symbols* (hence our mnemonic *cymbals*). The potential misinterpretation of the Eucharist as symbolic was known from the earliest times of the Church, and was always roundly condemned.

Conclusion: Ten Reasons and More to Give Thanks for Christ in the Eucharist

We have seen that Christ's words could hardly have been clearer, and the greatest voices of the Church could hardly have spoken in more complete agreement about Christ's Real Presence in his Body and Blood, soul and divinity in the sacrament of the Eucharist.

Indeed, even in the sixteenth century, the earliest and most influential Reformer, Martin Luther himself, defended the Real Presence and

18 Theodore of Mopsuestia, *Catechetical Homilies*, in Jurgens, *The Faith of the Early Fathers*, 2:82.

19 "In the light of modern scholarship it has become highly questionable whether he ought in any sense be regarded as a proponent, even an unwilling one, of Nestorianism." Jurgens, *The Faith of the Early Fathers*, 78.

wrote that all the Church Fathers affirmed it.[20] He rejected the Church's doctrine of *transubstantiation* that explained that Christ's body and blood are the *substance* of the consecrated Eucharist elements, while the *appearance* and all the sensible qualities or *accidents*, remain those of bread and wine. In its stead, he proposed his own philosophically unsound theory of *consubstantiation*, which maintained that the bread and wine contain the substance of Christ *along with* their natural substances. The doctrine of transubstantiation is an elegant and important one, a mystery beyond full human comprehension, and beyond the scope of this memory tour. For our purposes here, it will suffice to recall that even the greatest Reformer who dissented regarding the precise nature of Christ's Real Presence, would most likely thunder his disapproval at, and would likely rip down from their church doors, the prevalent, modern-day Protestant theses that flat-out deny Christ's Real Presence!

We've but scratched the surface of Christ's Real Presence, a presence that runs as deep as could possibly be into the very heart of the reality that God has so generously crafted for the purpose of our salvation. There are many more objections and reasons that could be learned and remembered,[21] many amazing Eucharist miracles still extant in our day,[22] but as much as there is to learn and contemplate on the topic of the Eucharist, we should never lose sight of the great miracle that occurs every day, perhaps at every second in some part of the world, when Christ is made present in the Eucharist in the holy sacrifice of the Mass. The Real Presence is not something merely to learn about, or even remember, but something, perhaps *the greatest thing*, that we can experience while on earth, with due reverence and gratitude, for as Christ himself has told us, "He who eats my flesh and drinks my blood abides in me, and I in him" (John 6:56).

---

20 Martin Luther, *Luther's Works* (St. Louis, MO: Concordia Publishing, 1961), 37:54.

21 For example, how the apparent contradiction to assert that Jesus was both bodily present at the Last Supper, while at the same time present in the bread and wine, is answered by an understanding of the difference between his *natural* and his *sacramental* presence.

22 See, for example, Joan Carroll Cruz's *Eucharistic Miracles* (Rockford, IL: TAN Books, 1987) for a discussion of miracles including that of a host and wine from the eighth century in Lanciano, Italy, that turned into visible flesh and blood. Still extant today, twentieth century tests have shown that the flesh is that of a human heart, and the blood is human, type AB.

About the Author

Kevin Vost (b. 1961) holds a Doctor of Psychology in Clinical Psychology (Psy.D.) degree from Adler University in Chicago. He has taught at Aquinas College in Nashville, the University of Illinois at Springfield, MacMurray College, and Lincoln Land Community College. Dr. Vost is the author of over a dozen Catholic books. He has served as a research review committee member for American Mensa, a society promoting the scientific study of human intelligence, and as an advisory board member for the International Association of Resistance Trainers, an organization that certifies personal fitness trainers. Dr. Vost drinks great drafts of coffee while studying timeless Thomistic tomes in the company of his wife, two sons, and their two dogs, in Springfield, Illinois. He welcomes questions or comments at his website: www.drvost.com.

Thank you for reading this book by Dr. Kevin Vost. We do hope you enjoyed it. En Route Books and Media invites you to also check out our other books available at www.enroutebooksandmedia.com.

CPSIA information can be obtained at www.ICGtesting.com
Printed in the USA
LVOW11s0851100416

482958LV00007B/725/P